M000306537

Rush of a Violent Wind

A Courageous Woman's Journey from Trauma through Psychological Transformation to Transcendence

James E. Gebhart, Ph.D.

Copyright © James E. Gebhart, 2018
Published by I_AM Self-Publishing, 2018.

The right of James E. Gebhart to be identified as the Author
of the Work has been asserted to them in accordance with the
Copyright, Designs and Patents Act 1988.

All rights reserved.

ISBN 978-1-912615-06-3

This book is sold subject to the condition it shall not, by way of
trade or otherwise, be circulated in any form or by any means,
electronic or otherwise without the publisher's prior consent.

@iamselfpub
www.iamselfpublishing.com

"Suddenly from heaven there came a sound like the rush of a violent wind, and it filled the entire house where they were sitting."

Acts of the Apostles, 2:1

The following non-fiction is an account of actual events in the life of a woman of extraordinary courage and resilience who experienced a redemptive cosmic vision.

Because the killer is still at large, some names, places and dates have been changed to protect the innocent.

Contents

1. Promise

Usually when the songbirds awakened her, Elaine would enjoy lying still and listening as they slowly formed a chorus. But this morning she sat up in bed with the immediate thought: "I will go down to the bakery just as it opens and get the cake."

She slipped out of bed, dressed quickly and moved to the porch. Looking up, she noticed the silver clouds drifting slowly toward Lake Michigan. Today was going to be wonderfully sunny and balmy. Walking slowly down the street, Elaine caught the scent of lilacs wafting from the bush at her corner curb. She appreciated her neighbors and the way they attended to their yards, weeding and grooming their irises, zinnias, lilies and coneflowers.

While admiring a coral rose bush in full bloom, she caught sight of Mrs. Lenahan, a woman in her fifties, kneeling in her garden, "Aren't you the ambitious one" she called with a smile.

Mrs. Lenahan turned, her startled expression softening. "Elaine, what a surprise. What brings you out this early?"

"I need ambitious friends like you. I don't have the patience for roses so I thought I would learn from an expert."

"They have a will of their own, believe me. And a history. Do you know I started this vine with a graft I took from my sister in California. That was six years ago. She is the one with the green thumb. But really Elaine, are you out for exercise or what?"

"No. I am going to the bakery. I want to be there when it opens. I have to pick up a surprise."

"Such a mystery."

"You will see. And of course you are going to drop by for brunch tomorrow, right?"

"Oh Elaine, I would love to. But I thought I might be in the way. The celebration is for Todd's graduation and all of his friends from school. It might be too crowded for us members of the old guard. And you have already been so good to me, helping me on a moment's notice with my grandchildren. And all the times you ran errands when . . . "

"Stop Ruth. You were specifically chosen to receive an invitation. And we have a reason for that. You will see."

"Even more mystery."

"Well, return to your garden. I would welcome a vase of fresh flowers tomorrow if you would be so kind."

"Count on it."

The bakery had just opened and one person was ahead of her, getting fresh bread, still warm. The baker was just "George" to her; if he had a last name she never knew it. He knew immediately why Elaine was there, held up a "one second" finger, went to the kitchen, then returned with the cake. "I confess I have never decorated one quite like this." Elaine studied it closely. A large rectangle of chocolate cake, more than enough for the crowd. It was covered with thick white icing, and across it in large red letters Elaine read CONGRADUATIONS DR. ATKINSON. And then down below was the word DAD flanking a small baby stroller in green and yellow. This would be the announcement.

Elaine smiled remembering how surprised Todd had been just four days ago when he had received the news that she was pregnant. It was shocking in its suddenness, coming right in the midst of his studies for his boards. He had stumbled to comprehend the reality. But last night he was clear. "A kiss for the baby" he said, kneeling in front of her belly. Elaine would never forget that moment. Now she could affirm herself with more self-esteem than she had ever known. This was a good marriage and a very good day.

George packed the cake in a special sling which made it easy to carry. She chose to return home by another street, this one canopied by trees: the maples and the flowering pears and the one great sycamore forming a border for a neighborhood that quietly commanded respect. The residences, mostly up-and-down duplexes, had retained their character: brick facing, pull-up windows, hardwood floors, and fine interior woodwork featuring built-in window seats. It was an area determined to persevere against the slow deterioration of its perimeter.

Just then a doleful and distant sound broke through the stillness and disrupted her mood. The train. The tracks a little over a mile away. It would be heading north or south, either way a grim and flinty path through abandoned dead-end streets and old shuttered brick buildings. A bleak and forbidding precinct of a calculating city. She frowned at the thought of how quickly the transition was from the gardens of Cullerton to the weedy ruins just to the east.

That ended her reverie. She hurried home. It was time for tea and toast. As she waited for the teapot she walked quietly into the bedroom, relaxing for a moment in an easy chair beside the still-sleeping Todd. His dear face had always elicited from her a warmth and trust. As she studied him carefully in his stillness she remembered the time a blind patient had truly wanted to "meet" him. The young woman had asked if she could sculpt his face for the genuine detail. Todd would always remember how she smiled as she traced his high jaw line, fine nose, lips and direct chin. Even in his modesty Todd had to admit that he had never felt more attractive.

And now they were going to start a family. Quite the sequel for two kids who had been impish friends in high school, then connecting in college. Her appreciation for Todd deepened over time as she was stimulated by his sense of humor and lack of pretense. And his creativity was impressive; he liked to stamp and tool leather for belts and wallets, and he made jewelry, having learned from casting gold crowns at school. It also helped that, as an Eagle Scout, he could repair most anything. And she was touched by his kindness; just a few days earlier he had stopped to change a flat tire for an older couple on the busy freeway. So typical.

The whistling teakettle summoned her to the kitchen. As the tea steeped she made the toast, found the jam, then the morning paper on the front porch. The noises reached Todd and she heard him rustle, then yawn. He always awakened slowly. So she took her breakfast back to the easy chair, opened the paper and perused the leads.

"So what greets our world this new day?"

"Let's see. This June 11, 1982. Well the Falklands War drudges on, a bizarre situation I still cannot understand. Great Britain at war with Argentina. Why on earth? What else? A Brazilian 727 has crashed into a mountain killing 135. Ugh, that's too grim to even think about. Want more? Israel's war with Syria continues. John Hinckley is still on trial for shooting Ronald Reagan." She tossed the paper on the table. "Enough. Enough. What else could go wrong?"

Todd stacked his pillows up and leaned back. "You know speaking of that subject, I have had Dad on my mind a lot. I think he's hanging on, just living for tomorrow. Afterwards it is going to be downhill. His Crohn's and the steroids have ruined his health."

"Don't worry so much about that. We'll have him over more often, and the baby will make him want to hold on."

He was now more pensive. "I'm not so confident. You just never know. Maybe that's why I bought that life insurance last month; in case something happens to me we will have some security, even after paying off all of the dental equipment."

She was impatient and breezy in her response. "As I've said before, that was a waste of money."

Todd looked at her for a long moment, then smiled broadly. And stretched again. "You're right. Enough of that. Up for my shower now."

He rolled out of bed and kissed the top of her head as he passed her chair. She returned to her breakfast. Except for the hiss of the shower it was quiet again. The meditative moment brought her attention to the wedding picture of two years ago which was framed and on the dresser. Here was the kind of ephemeral scene which studio photographers create in their shops, blending figures of Todd standing behind her, her head lilting back on his shoulder, a misty leafy tree in the background, and then emerging from the center the smaller silhouettes of the two of them, standing on a hillside, watching the sunrise of their future. Such a picture was unusual in her history. When she was growing up money was always scarce with little available for any film to document and record the lives of seven children. But everyone knew the real reason for the lack of photographs: mother would not risk being unfavorably compared to any other female.

The shower ended and Elaine heard Todd ask from his toweling: "Hey, what time do you expect Brian to get here?"

"Who knows? My brother will be late for his own funeral. He's always late. He said he hoped to get away at noon but that won't happen. He said he would be here by dinner, but he will be running late. It will probably be around midnight when we see him."

* * *

The sunny day should have been uplifting, but it could not penetrate his dark mood. Brian had not initially dreaded this trip. He wanted to see Laine and Todd; he loved them both dearly, was proud of Todd's accomplishment, and would be delighted if he were suddenly transported over to Chicago to be with them and celebrate. But driving all that way in his old blue Cutlass gave him too many hours with brooding. It was the same old review of the cascade of relentless stresses: the grind of his year of internship at the Madison Heights Family Chiropractic Center; the broken marriage and final separation; the money, almost exhausted; the endless fatigue. But the major stressor, the crippling one, was the premonition. For six months now he had had the most distinct sense that he was going to die soon. It came sometimes as an emerging shadow, other times as a sudden attack. He never knew around which corner the terror would be hiding. He was left with a pervasive feeling that would range from intense dread to frightened helplessness to occasional stoic resignation.

He had tried hard to understand this experience. He had known previous premonitions, or at least had always considered them such. But none like this. Philosophically he had always been interested in the paranormal, believing from an early age that far more is going on psychically than we fully understand. He had studied astral projections and had some success at actually telling people what they were wearing the night before. He had dabbled in palm reading and in automatic writing where he envisioned his "spirit guide" to be active. His grandmother and mother had been open to extra-sensory perception, and his interest in human energy fields and acupuncture strongly influenced his pursuit of training as a chiropractor. That had all been stimulating and provocative. But this weird feeling had turned into an ominous and terrifying regression.

He had thought about conveying his misgivings to Laine but decided to keep them to himself. Two years before, he had analyzed the Tarot cards as a glimpse into the future for Laine and Todd. However, the cards did not turn up well and in spite of his dismay he faithfully reported to them his prediction of a disaster they would face if they married. Laine was a free thinker, open to that which is beyond science, but was not overly disturbed by the Tarot reading, gently dismissing the matter while complimenting Brian for being a "Searcher." In the same way he imagined how she would have told him to just get himself to Chicago for the party, that all would go well.

However, now there was no alternative but to get started. He had waited too long already. Locking the front door, he walked down the sidewalk with the one suitcase and a brown bag gift for Laine that he knew she would like. He opened the trunk, put the suitcase in, and then came to a halt. He had forgotten that the spare tire was almost bald. Because he only drove around central Detroit, replacing it had not been a priority. But today would be much more than neighborhood transportation. He got down on the ground to once again inspect the worn steering. With that old spare it would be a big problem if he had tire trouble on this trip. And if he were to blow a front tire the steering might give way and he would lose control. He pushed on the wheel in an effort to detect any excessive looseness but could recognize nothing definite.

With a sigh he started the engine and slowly made his way west on Nine Mile Road through Oak Park, passing Providence Hospital, weaving his way to the Interstate. Finally he turned west onto I-96 only to find himself in a flood of cars and trucks. It seemed that literally everyone was tailgating or changing to what might be a faster lane. And all of their faces bore the stolid expression of person after person apparently enduring this return to the suburbs every working day. He shuddered. This was going to be an interminable trip.

* * *

Todd was out on an errand as Elaine sat at the dining room table preparing for tomorrow. On her left was an old maple hutch and a china cabinet which Todd's parents had kept in their attic. On the wall Todd had hung a clock he had made, encased in tooled leather featuring an eagle with a wide wingspread above an oak leaf patterns of acorns.

She had made a large platter of stuffed cabbage, some spaghetti and sauce, and a veggie tray. Elaine got dressed in one of her favorite shirts, a light blue baseball jersey designed by Todd's classmates. It had the Illinois-Chicago School of Dentistry logo on the front, and the words: DRILL EM FILL EM BILL EM on the back. They had joked about how the words were not only appropriate for dentists for also for gigolos.

There were far more napkins, cups, plates and supplies than would be needed. Around a dozen people were expected for coffee, juice, bagels and doughnuts before the commencement service: Todd's parents, his brother and wife, Elaine's mother, two sisters, a couple of friends, Brian, Mrs. Lenahan, and perhaps two or three classmates. Then after commencement maybe another fifteen classmates and friends over for entrees, sandwiches, punch, and cutting the large cake on the dining room table. She cut the cardboard box so as to reveal only the upper half of the cake. CONGRADUATIONS DR. ATKINSON would be apparent, but the lower half would be unveiled at the moment of the announcement of the baby. Even Todd would be surprised. And how would mother react?

Where to put all the people? They could mill about the living room, dining room and kitchen. The sofa for three people, the lounge chair, the two window seats, the end chair from the study, six dining room chairs, two folding chairs and the desk chair. Guests would pass the two small bedrooms on the left to reach the bathroom between them. Elaine closed the door to their bedroom which was difficult to make tidy, overfilled with the waterbed, dresser, easy chair and a small end table. Hanging over the bed, depicting a bullfighter, was a small rug, hooked by Elaine's sister Shirley. She left the back bedroom door open. It had been converted to a study and the guests were welcome to imagine her hard-working husband sitting at that large desk which covered most of one wall, or note the bookshelf which Todd's father had made now overflowing with six years of text books, stacks of paper and journals.

They would make do. They could all park behind the apartment and Todd could lead the small caravan to the university. Even though it would be a Friday morning, Elaine did not want anyone to stray into the rough neighborhoods.

Todd soon returned with the packages of ham, cheese, turkey, lettuce, mayonnaise and bread. They must remember to pick up ice on the way back from commencement. Elaine took the borrowed punch bowl from its box in the corner and put it on the kitchen counter. She could quickly mix the ingredients when guests arrived.

Todd stepped outside and sat on the front steps. The porch thermometer read 63 degrees. The sun would soon begin to set in the west, the ending of a most pleasant day. Brian would have no weather problems and his trip should be easy. But he would be late. Hearing music from upstairs Todd remembered that Chip was having a party that night. He and Elaine would be more than welcome to drop in at any time. That might be fun. He would certainly know all of the students and the relief of finals being a thing of the past would be a contentment common to everyone.

Elaine appeared at the door, then joined him. "I think everything is almost in order. Imagine our being so organized."

Todd stretched and smiled. "What's for dinner?"

"Gosh, I forgot all about that!" She laughed. "How about some Ramen noodles?"

* * *

The Interstate led due west past Dearborn Heights, slowed to a crawl near Livonia, then merged to a crowded racetrack as it approached the Airport Express Outer Belt. Above Brian roaring aircraft made their way to a final approach at Detroit Metropolitan. Around him on both sides massive trucks intensified his tension and his increasing headache. He thought for a moment about symptoms of a brain tumor, then impatiently dismissed the thought as ridiculous. His route tied in, finally, with Rt. 14, the old road to Ann Arbor. The afternoon was already beginning its descent as the city landscape now melted into the shadowed fields and huddled hills.

Brian tried to settle into a routine for the trip, seeking to clear his mind. He thought of Laine, his little sister. Actually she was only three years younger, but he was always just enough ahead of her to be the "big" brother, sometimes her protector, always her support. When she went through all the terrible times with mother in that other room, he would try to be there for her afterwards, to comfort her. But the memory of that pain brought him back to his own, the headache now keeping time to the rhythmic thumping of the wheels crossing the concrete connectors. The pulsation, mile after mile. And he thought he detected a vibration in the steering, a shimmy in the right front wheel. Or could it be the ball joint, slowly eroding from the tremors of the highway?

Just west of Ann Arbor he joined I-94, the literal lower belt of Michigan, wrapping across the state from Lake Huron in Canada to Benton Harbor on the dunes of Lake Michigan. Brian was prepared for it to be busy as it was the only possible route to the west for trucks. But he was not anticipating the construction from Jackson to Battle Creek. Traffic was restricted to two lanes, and for over twelve miles the orange barrels loomed just a few feet away from his right door while the massive tires of the tractor trailers rolled by just off his left shoulder. With the unrelenting tension, his dull headache spread down his neck and into his shoulders.

The sky was now a dying violet, the horizon liver-colored. He turned on the radio and searched for music, to find some mellow place which would transport him back to better times of dance and laughter and friends. But there was nothing. He slowed down to sixty to ease the burden on the steering, only to be caught up in the wash of seemingly every truck and car passing him on the left, some casting irritable looks at him for his slower speed. He sighed, rubbed his neck, and reached for some Tylenol.

When the construction finally ended Brian became aware of the ache in his hands and arms from his grip on the steering wheel, and beads of sweat on his forehead. He wanted to stop and rest, but it was already too late and that would be foolish. Time to get hold of himself, to stop this downward spiral of worry and dread. He caricatured himself as a neurotic, someone emotionally crippled to some significant degree. That only added to his depression and his growing fatigue.

A sign near Kalamazoo announced that Chicago was 210 miles ahead. He began to concentrate on taking deep, easy, slower breaths, seeking a rhythm to the passing miles. But the rhythm began to take the form of drifts toward sleep, and this commanded hyper-alertness. He found a talk-radio station, thinking new ideas would be stimulating. But the callers seemed stupid and the host was a raging narcissist. He could only persist. Mile after mile after endless mile.

Far ahead he watched the dim glow of what would be the lights of Benton Harbor at midnight and he took satisfaction that he was moving into the final leg of this ordeal. But the fatigue was having its effect. Across the green median the lights of the eastbound traffic began to string together in a hazy blur, a long line of tapioca bobbing and flowing past him. When he would take off his glasses to clean them he would quickly lose all focus. He would just have to make do with the cloudy glare. He concentrated on his own side of the turnpike, but the blurring repeated, this time all the red tail lights bubbling up like drops of blood on a long, deep abrasion. He was driving slower and passing traffic flashed their brights at him, pronouncing him a hazard.

Brian had to get out of the Cutlass. He pulled into a truck stop just a few miles north of Indiana. Walking around in the cool night air, he found the bathroom, splashed water on his face, and then sat down at a far corner booth for hot tea and blessed quietness. A waiter walked by with a grilled cheese sandwich and Brian pointed to it and nodded, suddenly wanting one for himself. Maybe he should not have gone all day without food. But with this pause and clarity came the compelling belief that he should not continue, that he must, right now, call Laine and say that he was not feeling well and would be turning back. He checked his pocket change and looked around for the pay phone.

But wait. This was really crazy. What was he to do, sleep in his car for a few hours then turn around and drive all the way back to Detroit? And with only an hour or so to Laine's? All of this upheaval from that damned premonition, some inner seismic meter that announced an imminent tsunami. What made him think that the secrets and energy of the world around him could find their unique channel through him, and he would be one of the few who knew their codes? Just plain crazy. But on the other hand, he believed in his deeply-felt experiences, in his ability to detect danger as a dog accurately senses fear. What are intuition, and instinct, and the truth of dreams and visions, archetypes and ancient memories? Surely a force existed which impacted events, and perhaps it could be said that he had mustered the courage to directly confront such dread.

He sat in his private world for some twenty minutes. Twice he reached for change for the phone. Then it occurred to him that the disaster he feared might not be scheduled for his trip to Chicago but on his return to Detroit. So there was no comfort to be found in turning back, and perhaps he was mistaken all around.

With that thought, he paid the waitress, checked the tires, and then aimed the dark blue Cutlass west toward Chicago.

* * *

The party upstairs sounded lively. The laughter, the shuffling of dance, the heavy beat of the music. Todd and Elaine smiled and talked about it. Chip was a real good guy, had worked hard to stay ahead of his studies, and had dreamed of this ending. They were deserving of their celebration.

"We could go up there and join them. Wouldn't have to stay too long. Just nip their booze and snacks and tell a good story or two about Chip."

Elaine wrinkled her nose. "Yeah. I wish we could. But I better stay here by the phone in case Brian calls. He could be here any time. I am so damned tired, I was hoping to be asleep hours ago. Where is that boy? But you could go up for a while if you want."

"Nah. I don't need a hangover. I will wait here with you."

They curled on the sofa for a while, listening to the celebration upstairs. They wondered when someone dropped something heavy, sounding as if it did not break but splashed all over things. Then Elaine said: "I forgot to tell you that mother called. She and Shirley are leaving about 6:30 in the morning. I had to give directions again for how to get to Cullerton."

"Maybe she will get lost. Or abducted by aliens."

"If only we could be so lucky."

Elaine looked at Todd from the side as he lay there, his eyes closed, his fingers drumming to the rhythm of party music. He was the only person she had ever told about surviving mother as a child, and Todd despised that woman ever after. But he kept his fury deep in his inner fortress, and was forever civil, bearing the private burden of the knowledge.

"Dear Mommy will feign delight and find a way to be the center of attention. Brian will squirm at that, but what else can he do. And speaking of Brian, he is pushing the limits this time."

"I can't imagine that anything has happened. He is just being Brian. Are you truly worried?"

"No, we would have heard. He probably has a note pinned to his coat which reads *In case of emergency notify Elaine Atkinson at the following number*. We would have heard. Unless he drove into Lake Michigan."

"Weird. Nothing we can do but wait."

In a while Todd gently dozed off. Elaine could not sleep and listened as the party upstairs gradually moved toward its conclusion. One person coming down the stairs, another car door outside shutting, another car starting. All were respectful of the neighbors and keeping the noise to a minimum. And finally ending.

It was now 2:30 A.M. She had assumed they would all three have been asleep by this time, ready to arise at dawn, prepare breakfast, and get ready for the wonderful day. She felt a wave of anger for Brian's lack of consideration. But this was followed by a voice of compassion, reminding her of his troubled marriage, his difficulties at school, and how, like her, he had struggled throughout his childhood. With these thoughts and the recollection of all the times Brian had watched over her and encouraged her, all was forgiven.

Only the mantra remained: "Come on, Brian. Get here safely. I want you with us on this day."

* * *

The distant glow of Chicago had a soothing effect. The tension began to melt, the headache subside. His focus changed. It was going to be an enormous relief to see her in the doorway.

Interstate 94 merged briefly with other expressways, then began its long and distinctive curve around the base of Lake Michigan. He was very familiar with the exits to Gary and Hammond. He knew by heart the direct route to Laine. It was very late but the traffic was moderately heavy as he passed Calumet City and he began the straight arrow vector to downtown and the exit to Laine's.

Brian turned onto Cermak, over through Dvorak Park, then right on Leavitt. Finally he eased into the drive at 2301 Cullerton, noticing the front porch and living room lights on at Laine's. He cut the engine and sat in silence for more than a minute. There remained a roaring in his ears, an ache in his arms and back, and remnants of the perceptual tilting that had remained with him since awakening in the morning. But this was real. He was here now, in this driveway, all was quiet, and Laine and Todd were in that room.

She heard the sound of the car door in the driveway and at first let it pass, thinking it was another of Chip's guests leaving his party. Then she sat up. His party was over. Her words rang out and awakened Todd. "I think he is here!" She ran to the door and there was Brian himself, trudging up the sidewalk, a suitcase in one hand, a bag in the other.

"I am a little late" he said sheepishly.

"Why it's only 3 A.M." And Elaine threw her arms around him, and then Todd joined the embrace.

"What took so long? Car trouble?"

"No, it took me a while to get out of town. I had to say goodbye to Sharon, the kids and a few friends. And hey, your place looks good! Look at that cake! And, oh yeah, I brought you this."

Elaine opened the brown bag and lifted a bottle of Jack Daniels Black Label.

"Still your favorite I presume, but beyond the budget of a graduate student and his wife."

"It was my favorite. But I can't drink it now."

"Why? Are you pregnant or something?" An offhand remark, and then the odd silence and the slow awakening.

"Laine? Really?"

She nodded and they embraced again and again. The thrill was effervescent, energized by the enormous relief Brian felt at having arrived safely, innervated by their laughter, and now pulsating with the news of Laine expecting a baby. Laine and Todd having a baby! The reality brought a flood of memories, many of them back to their childhood years when Laine would play mother with her dolls and Brian would tease her that she would put them in cradles in the treetop and drop them all on their heads. Or that she would turn into a shrieking witch of a mother and her children would all run away. He reminded her of those times and she adored him for it. And then he hugged her again. Laine felt as if she were cocooned in joy.

2. Horror

Their excitement carried them forward for over an hour until the final arrival of heavy fatigue. It was already 4:30 and guests would be arriving by 8:30. Todd made quick calculations and decided that they had better go get the doughnuts now, then come back and get maybe three hours of sleep.

"Come with me Brian. It is only six blocks to the bakery."

"Todd, please, don't go to that place. Not at this hour. Go to the one over in Little Italy."

Todd nodded and left with Brian. Of course he was not going to drive two miles when fresh doughnuts were right around the corner. As they pulled into the parking lot, he did note why Elaine would recoil. The red neon light was broken, part of it hanging limp. Parking lot lighting did not even reach the edges of the property. An adjacent dry cleaning establishment had gone out of business. But they were here and through the open car windows he could already smell the yeasty first trays of new doughnuts just out of the oven.

Two or three early patrons, presumably regulars but rough looking, were sitting at tables, one reading the paper. Todd ordered a dozen doughnuts, a dozen bagels, and a carton of cream cheese. Brian became aware that one man was looking over his paper and watching Todd very carefully as he purchased the food. And the same dark turbulence that had almost crushed him all the way over from Detroit was present again, waves of fear that were gathering to pull him under. He started to speak of it to Todd, then checked himself. He would appear crazy. As Todd casually took the packages and started for the car, Brian could hardly get his legs to move. He looked backward as they walked, searching the dark parking lot for any movement. They got in the car, started the engine, and finally drove away. Brian closed his eyes, took a deep breath, and noticed that he was wet with sweat.

By 5 a.m. they were back at the house, ready for bed. Elaine said that she would just stay up, that it would not be possible for her to function on just two hours of sleep. Todd shrugged, jumped into a quick shower, and then to bed. Brian followed with his own shower and deflected Elaine's request to help him open the sofa to the hide-a-bed. He would simply sleep on the sofa. She gave him a pillow and two sheets, then turned the light out in the living room. Brian was asleep almost instantly.

The expanse of sudden quietness brought Elaine to a sense of her own deep weariness. She thought of sleep again but quickly overruled it. For now she would brew some tea and set up the sandwich trays for the luncheon gathering. As she worked she was aware of the birds beginning to sing.

She had previously decided there would be no decorations, but now began to reconsider. In the boxes under the dining room table were materials that could be used: stars to be pinned, rolls of crepe paper for streamers, even some small balloons which could be clustered. She knelt down on the floor, examining the idea.

It was then that she heard the sound. She looked to her right, thinking it was the cat. She looked back to her left and froze. There, just three feet away, were two black shoes. Looking up she found that the shoes attached to two legs in black jeans. Lifting her head she saw the black gun aimed at her face. A gun with a man. Her stare was fixed on the barrel of the gun and she could not or dare not make eye contact with the dark face above it.

In this moment it was as if her very self, her soul, split into two components: the apocalyptic and the reflective. On the one side was the eruption of her screaming, screams she could not stop, and in the cacophony the intruder was shouting for her to "shut up, shut up, shut up you bitch!" On the other side was a detached analytical curiosity, measuring the equation, wondering "Doesn't he see the cake on the table, that we are getting ready for a party, and doesn't he realize that you don't take a gun to a party?"

He was dragging her by the hair toward the living room when Brian suddenly appeared in the doorway. Now the terrified screams were joined by the roaring of the gun, flashing and exploding again and again and again. And from her scientific side came the question: "Why is he shooting Brian? Brian has just awakened to this nightmare, has come in to see what is happening. He is standing there in his underwear, confused. He doesn't even have his glasses on. He is no threat."

The first two rounds pierced Brian's abdomen and as he fell, he shouted out for Todd. Elaine struggled to reach her brother when the man stood over Brian and took careful aim, firing one more round into his chest. From one side of her soul shrieked the unimaginable horror; from the other side came the analytic observation: "He has a smile on his face. He is getting off on this!"

Brian had called out to warn Todd, and now the man turned his attention to the bedroom and walked toward it. Elaine lunged at him, grabbing his arm, trying to pull him back as he walked across the room and opened the bedroom door. Todd was just sitting up in bed, being transported in moments from a deep sleep to a bewildering war zone in the other room. The man raised the black gun and from three feet away put a bullet through Todd's skull, entering above the right temple and lodging in his left jaw. Todd pitched forward limp onto his pillow.

Reality now began to fragment as time and space and orientation no longer fit. With fistfuls of her hair being viciously wrenched, Elaine found herself being hauled out of the bedroom. He was demanding money even as he searched Todd's wallet. Her endless screaming on the one hand clashed oddly with her analytic observation that this monster cannot possible appreciate the beauty of that wallet which Todd tooled from fine natural leathers, trimmed in black leather, and completed with engravings of peacocks on the back. Then into focus came Brian, on the floor. He was grey, gaping like a grappled fish on a dock. She moved toward him to help. Brian indicated that he wanted to sit up somehow, perhaps to increase his breathing, so she pulled him up with his back against the T.V. But the man kicked her away, searching for Brian's wallet. Elaine then rushed back to Todd only to stop short of touching him. He was like a slab of meat that had been slammed to the wall, raw, seeping. His eyes were open but empty, sightless. His breathing was shallow, raspy, blood bubbling from his lips and streaming from his ear. The blood was everywhere. She looked up at the hooked rug, the bullfighter hanging over the bed, now splattered red. And speckled with grey matter.

Then he was back, grabbing her hair again, demanding that she take him to her car and drive him away. In some feeble attempt to be logical she weakly uttered "No. You have shot them both. Just take the car and leave." To which he jerked her hard by the hair, put the gun in her face, and told her she would do as he said. Again the split within her. One side of her was crying in a state beyond all hysteria, overwhelmed by the incomprehensible carnage and pain, plummeting into helplessness. But the other side sized him up, concluding "No, he won't just leave. If I go with him he will rape me and then kill me. If I stay he will kill me. So survival is not an option. I belong here with Todd and Brian." And so she dug her feet and elbows into the corner of the foyer by the front door, refusing to be dragged away, and for the first time looked him directly in the eye and said it: "You mother fucking bastard."

At this the man stopped, looked her in the eye for a silent moment, then slowly pointed the black gun at her face, and pulled the trigger. Nothing happened. He had used up all of his rounds. So he raised the steel weapon and struck her in the head, again and again until she dropped into some kind of oblivion. When she regained consciousness, she found herself being dragged across the front porch toward her car. With a sudden surge of immense energy she wrenched herself free, screaming for help, and began to run into the house for the telephone. He seized her again and was pulling her back from the front door when the dogs next door started barking. He stopped, swore, then turned and ran off.

Elaine heard the sirens as she stumbled back to her house. Returning to the scene from the outside was a new horror. The floors were slick with blood. Brian was cadaver grey, sweating, gasping for his next breath, trying to crawl across the living room. Her instinct was to just lie down beside him and hold him. She was assuring him that help was on the way when she heard his raspy whisper: "Laine, go be with your husband."

When she was away from Todd, Elaine shifted into some mode of thinking that Todd was badly wounded but would manage to survive, but when she entered his room she was suddenly faced with the grim reality. She listened to him gasp for breath, spoke to him softly that help was coming, and managed to touch him gently. Then she noticed that great pools of blood had gathered on the water bed, clear down to his knees. She felt paralyzed, destitute, and again aware of the sirens in the distance but not really believing that they would ever arrive. And she watched Todd take each shuddering breath, wondering if it might be his last.

The police appeared suddenly, storming the house with guns drawn, shouting commands. With the cover clear the medical team entered, quickly assessed Brian and took immediate steps to transport him to the nearest hospital. She noticed that they shook their heads when making a quick assessment of Todd, and began to attend to her. For the first time Elaine realized that she was bleeding profusely from her scalp wounds. Her blood was mixed with all the other blood on the floors.

Elaine felt the room spinning around as everyone rushed about, evaluating the situation, searching inside and outside for answers. Then Chip appeared at the door, having been awakened from what he first thought to be a nightmare brought about by too much alcohol at his party. He had locked his door and hidden until the police arrived.

The ambulance crew requested that Elaine ride with them as they took Brian to the hospital. She said that she would follow shortly, that for now she needed to be with Todd. A police officer came and stood between her and Todd's room, gravely shaking his head. Chip came to her side and took her hand. Elaine looked up at both and lifted the question "Is he dead?" They both nodded yes. Her lament began to trail off. "Oh Jesus! Oh Jesus! Oh Jesus."

3. Wake

She was placed on a gurney in the large room. Next to her, behind a curtain, the medical staff was working to stabilize Brian. He would repeatedly scream which, though horrifying, she welcomed as proof that he was still alive. She felt herself at the epicenter of a vortex, an eruption of shattered shards of life. She imagined that the hospital itself would be lifted up and carried away.

After only a few minutes Brian was wheeled off to some other place. Now Elaine was alone and everything seemed so distant. The sirens, the smells, the mad rushing about felt detached from her. Voices echoed in the distance. Even her own words seemed to be robotic, disconnected. She glanced at the round or long faces without any sense of recognition. Her own skin looked odd, felt cold and dry, reptilian. The hospital smelled of an acrid blend of disinfectants and fouled cloth. Her hospital gown gaped in the back, a ludicrous foreign costume.

At her bedside an impatient young doctor kept trying to persuade her that an X-ray was recommended. Her skull did not appear fractured but X-rays were required to assess any damage within. And when she had simply refused because of her pregnancy, he then kept trying to educate her that the X-ray would have no effects on her baby. His words faded away in the confusion.

Why had all three of the nurses been tearful? Had the ambulance crew spread the word? About her husband and brother too? One nurse kept apologizing that she had to shave Elaine's head for the sutures, to cut away her beautiful hair. Why are they concerned about that? Her hair no longer mattered. A final scalping.

She thought of the chaplain who had come by. He alone did not try to talk, to explain things. His presence was the quiet center of the storm. He was there for just a few minutes until he was interrupted. She remembered his eyes: kind but reflecting the immense sorrow of this place.

Her head throbbed. But once again she refused medication. A piece of Todd still lived within her and she would protect it. And her defiance now mobilized some central core. She needed to stand on her own feet, to diffuse the pain flashing from her legs and hips, her shoulder and arm, and her head. The haven of unreality was now fading, and she focused again on the maelstrom.

"Can you tell me anything about my brother, Brian Preston? I don't hear him anymore." The nurse turned around, startled by Elaine's new lucidity, quickly moving her IV from the gurney to an IV cart. Then returning to the vital question: "He is in surgery. We will come and report to you just as soon as we know anything."

Elaine mustered a weak smile of appreciation for the moment of kindness, an expression that was immediately noticed by the two detectives in the corner. They arose from their chairs and she studied them as they approached. The older one was tall, a bit stooped, thin and swarthy with a prominent brow framing the permanent sadness in his eyes. His suit was grey, his tie a faded blue. A grey man. The other was of average height, athletic build, thick brown hair, assertive in his movement, quick and detailed in his scanning. He had on a plaid sport jacket and a maroon turtle neck shirt. They seemed slightly menacing, standing by her bed, wanting to recall any possible detail about the man's description: height, weight, color of skin, clothing, mannerisms, voice features, any evidence of his being on drugs. Elaine tried to help but that effort took her back to her house and the horror. She fought the memories. Their questions were pulling her back to a world she wanted to escape. She did not want to remember that face . . . his arm . . . the enormous gun in his hand . . . the menacing smile when he shot Brian in the chest. She closed her eyes, momentarily blocking the police voices and the urgent need for information. Moving away, far away.

The nurse came to adjust her I.V. and the detectives had to excuse themselves. Thankful for the privacy she lay back on the gurney, turning to her side, slipping into her cradle, searching for a sanctuary from the clamor all around, the metallic voices, the perpetual commotion reverberating in her pounding headache. The room began to slowly tilt as the surge increased beyond all limits. It was urgent that she find a way to steady herself, to detach from this chaos and madness. Her only focus was on the drop of water from the hanging bag as it breached the space down to the tube that would take it to her arm. Each drop was stretching, elongating until finally breaking loose in its plunge. Time was much slower now. And then she found the exit light at the far door, a soft beam as if filtered through the water, hazing the room. Water and light. Yes, we are all mostly water. Flesh is vulnerable, but not water. And the light that glides across the water. Gliding from an easy wind, like her single breath. One slower breath followed by another, and then another still deeper. From the depths comes the moving air to push the sails over the water, to transport her away from this place, from this morning in history, from this battered body. Yes, to drift upon the water, through the misty light, to a place far, far away. Where it is silent. And calm. And peaceful.

Her trance, her refuge, was suddenly disrupted by someone in a white coat, besieging her again with medicines for her headache. Or was it her insanity? This nurse pulled her back to her ravaged body, to the waters of herself. And she was immediately seized by the mad release of an explosive diarrhea.

The nurse's personal cleaning brought Elaine's full attention to the present. She seized upon details. It was nearly 8:15. Todd's parents were driving up from Gary and meeting at Carl's house to drive over for the party together. Someone had to reach them before they got to the house. Someone had to redirect them.

Now Elaine realized that she must not succumb to any kind of stupor or trance. She must cooperate with the police or that man would drift away forever. She looked across the room at the detectives who came to her. "Where is my husband now?"

The older one, the sad one, answered with precise directness. "He is still at the house. The investigation must be thorough, including photographs and a careful analysis of every detail. I understand that he will very soon be transported to the coroner."

The house. The house. The vision returning. The memory seen now through chips of shattered lenses. The screaming and explosions. The cake on the dining room table. Birdsong. The kitchen. The gun with the man. The blood everywhere. Brian trying to crawl across the living room, trying to breathe. The pool of blood around Todd's knees. Chip. The bullfighter rug. The killer's hand in her hair, dragging her to the door. The ambulance. Brian, in surgery now. Why did he need to shoot anyone?

She turned quickly to the detectives, now becoming the interrogator. "What happened? Where did he come from? What did he want? Where is he?"

The tall one studied her for a moment, then framed his words. "We are investigating and need to get as much information as we can to answer those questions."

She returned to the target. "How did he get in? Why us? Why the gun?"

A pause and a chosen breath. "It appears he kicked in a plywood window in the basement, the one with the hole in it for the clothes dryer exhaust. As to why he picked you, we need to know that. Does he resemble anyone you have seen before?"

This was followed by a barrage of questions, queries, theories. About known enemies. Persons who might have reason to wish anyone ill will. Anything of great value in the house? Any associations with the drug world? Any serious debt to anyone? The questions continued.

She interrupted, shaking her head." "Why didn't I die?" At this both detectives paused, then spoke: "Is there any reason he should have killed you? Or spared you in particular?"

A lengthy silence followed. "We know this is difficult for you. We are here to help. . ."

"Just get him."

* * *

As she lay on the gurney in the emergency room she was quietly attended by the nurses and detectives. But the calm would be short-lived. The noisy flurry of the group coming down the hall would have been distracting in itself, but when she heard the familiar voice she opened her eyes to full alert and took a deep breath.

Mother entered the room with Elaine's sister Shirley obediently following behind. Mother, large framed and broad abeam, quickly assessed Elaine, taking command like a drill sergeant. "You look terrible" was her first remark, and then, quickly, to deflect any discourse, she ordered "You will stay with me tonight at your Uncle Robert's." No further words or gestures of concern. No reference to Todd or Brian.

Mother then moved to the edge of the gurney, monitoring the remainder of the IV, and began the recitation of her own trauma – how she and Shirley had arrived from Gary only to find Cullerton all but blocked off by police cars. She had parked and walked immediately to Elaine's house where she had to stop at the curb. When she identified herself an officer was called over and reported the shooting. She related in detail her frustrations of the morning. "They would not let me in the house. My own son-in-law. Me, a nurse. They would not even let me use the bathroom. It was outrageous."

Elaine positioned herself as she had done for years, looking over mother's shoulder, hearing but not responding, detached while vigilant. Mother in her typical form, asked the nurse for a glass of water, then scowled when she was given directions to the drinking fountain.

Shirley wondered who should be notified. Mother decided. "I don't think we should bother calling Beverly. She would not come anyway."

Although confronting mother was almost always an invitation to a volatile scene, at this time Elaine felt required to intervene. "If it looks like Brian might die then she should have that opportunity."

Mother eyes now locked on Elaine's in their first engagement. The reference to the possibility of Brian dying was a reality now that it had been spoken. And Beverly would be a problem. Mother had not spoken to her daughter Beverly for over six years, and there seemed to be no reason to add that stress to the scene. Elaine found herself momentarily disgusted by mother's dilemma. Mother, who over the years alternated from daughter to daughter as to who would next be exiled.

A nurse appeared to disconnect the IV and note the same on the medical chart. She then unstrapped Elaine from the gurney and gave her a tee shirt that someone had found for her. It was from some rock concert, a group Brian would probably recognize. It was also too large but would have to suffice because her own bloodied shirt was being kept by the police as evidence. Mother and Shirley then stood back as the detectives re-entered the room, explaining that Elaine was soon to be discharged and would then need to go to the morgue to identify the body. This made no sense to Elaine as everyone knew all that had happened. The detectives explained that the first responders had been replaced by new personnel at the house, and that in a criminal case a positive identification would be required in the coroner's presence.

Elaine was staggered by this sudden development. The very idea of looking upon Todd's body re-opened the pictures in her mind of the house and the bedroom, scenes she was trying to lock away. Todd, once again, helpless and limp as a dog struck by a car, sucking final bloody breaths of a now fractured and mindless life. So it was expected that she would simply face this reality. And this was followed by another prospect even more unacceptable, that mother would take her to the coroner's, and, worse, would take charge of the identification. Mother who held Todd in contempt because he was a man and one who made no attempt to placate her, while Todd privately detested mother. This must not happen.

She excused herself to the privacy of the emergency room bathroom, creating a bit of time and space for some plan. She could manage to overhear the conversation in the room which was now of detailed interest to her. Some friends and family had arrived in the waiting room and she wanted to avoid their condolences. Todd's parents had been taken to Carl's house, but Carl's wife Juanita was here. Juanita. That would work. Juanita would volunteer to drive. That would be logical. Todd had always found his sister-in-law interesting, incredibly mechanical and strong-willed, and so unfeeling. The mystery was why his brother ever married her. But now she would be helpful. And Juanita would quite readily agree. Going to the coroner's would be no different for her than fulfilling a Saturday errand.

Walking was difficult and returned her attention to the pain which had spread from her legs and hips, to her shoulder and arm. Signs of the deep bruising were already appearing. Stepping outside into the midmorning sunshine brought her back to the ongoing world, people driving around on a routine day. Two men were standing by their car in the parking lot, laughing at something, enjoying the moment. As she walked by them she glared, expressing the irrational feeling that they had no right to be so irreverent.

Elaine settled gingerly into the car as Juanita confidently moved out toward her objective. The traffic was lifeless, mechanical, and she turned her eyes to the sky where the clouds were hanging, pure white, soft as Todd's shaving cream. But they seemed to be alive, and she watched as two began to converge, now becoming a large, folded drape. A shroud. The lonely vigil began.

The coroner's office was not very far from Rush Hospital. Juanita was quiet, unemotional. Elaine was aware that Juanita had responded not so much because she felt the urge to help but rather because she found the task interesting. Typical Juanita, satisfied to fit pieces of daily puzzles together. Elaine turned away, looking at the campus. As she did, there slowly came into view all of the activity over at the Pavilion of the Illinois-Chicago campus. Something familiar there. Yes, the caps and gowns. Just like Todd's. Oh God, it actually was Todd's graduating class! Commencement was apparently over; graduates and families were coming, milling around, taking joyous pictures. She then remembered that she had put new film in her camera yesterday for this moment, at that very place.

Her eyes were closed when the car stopped at the morgue. But Elaine was still back at the Pavilion, posing with Todd in his cap and gown, now a picture of Todd and his proud parents. And the festive congratulations, the talk of opening a dental practice, the caricatures of this professor in his academic regalia and that professor still lecturing to a small group about some current issue. Juanita called her back to task and was then surprised when Elaine said "You are going to have to do this. I just can't." Juanita studied her for a moment, then quietly agreed, left the car and walked directly to the building. Elaine had no idea how long she sat alone in the car. Time was disconnecting again. She imaged Todd's graduation gown still in the closet at the house, the sandwiches in the refrigerator ready for brunch. And Brian, so fearful of coming for the party. And the hooked rug over Todd's bed, the bloody bullfighter. And the pulsating currents of pain traversing so many bones of her body.

Juanita finally returned to the car and, by way of report, simply remarked "I've completed the authentication."

* * *

Upon arriving back at the hospital, Elaine found her family in the waiting room of Intensive Care. Brian was out of surgery but his condition remained critical. Mother dramatically reported the facts. They had removed part of his liver, part of a lung, and some of his intestines. One shot had nicked his aorta, just a half inch away from his heart. Two bullets were removed from his abdomen and one from his chest. They discovered another fragment in his arm and this was mysterious since no entry wound in his arm could be found. It had to have been a ricochet from one of the other bullets. The surgery had required several hours and multiple blood transfusions. Now only time would tell.

As mother began to organize and schedule the rest of the day, Elaine managed to excuse herself to go to the restroom. As she came out she was met again by the detectives with their questions. They studied her intently. She was aware that some of the questions had been asked before, but maybe they were checking for consistency. There were discrepancies. The shorter detective was confrontational: "You have two different reports on how tall the attacker was. He probably was around the same height as your brother. The taller perspective probably came because you were on the floor looking up at him." Elaine shrugged. "But then what about this. One time you say his shoes were black, his pants were black, his skin was dark black. Later you say the shoes were white sneakers, he was wearing blue jeans, and he had a tan complexion. How can that be?" Elaine found herself responding almost as if in free association. "Black. Black. Everything about him was black. Black face. Black jeans. Black gun. Like a black hole. A sucking black hole surrounded by a glowing brightness. I know it doesn't make sense but I saw it both ways." The detectives looked at one another, then said something about taking her back with them to the house the next day or two for more details. And that was a thought she could not tolerate just now.

Fatigue was having its effect from the longest day of her life. She stepped outside for fresh air and was met by a reporter from *The Chicago Tribune*. She later found it hard to believe that she could or would submit to an interview. The news team promised not to display her picture but eagerly seized every word she could offer. Perhaps she was motivated by the need to get the word out so that some kind of public dragnet might help find the killer. Perhaps it was cathartic, to have the world know just how bloody and horrible it was to be in that room and what that man had done. Perhaps it was the sight of that graduating class at the Pavilion where Todd should have been. Perhaps it was her own loss, and though she was historically a very private person she found herself telling of learning of the pregnancy just last Monday, that she and Todd had picked out a name for a boy and a name for a girl, and now the baby would never know the father. Later, when she read the story, she was surprised to read what she had said.

* * *

The late afternoon hour required that arrangements be made for the night. Mother took care of the matter, having already called her brother Robert and his wife Louise in LaGrange. In her exhaustion Elaine succumbed to passivity, just doing what she was told. But when mother began to insist on the importance of taking a sleeping pill, she again was aroused to resistance, refusing all medication because of the baby. All the way to Uncle Robert's she endured the harping of both mother and Shirley about the need for food – "you must eat for the baby" – and the need for rest. She was not at all hungry, but the escape of sleep beckoned.

Uncle Robert's house looked pleasant and comfortable: in the living room a round, weathered oak coffee table was surrounded on one side by a tan sofa of soft cloth and accented throw pillows, and on the other two colorful striped end chairs. The fireplace was painted white, inviting guests to come and study the family portraits on the mantle. The silence was awkward as no one knew what they could possibly say or do. There was news that Elaine seized upon and found touching, that the word of Todd's death had spread as his classmates assembled for graduation. They spontaneously chose to leave his chair empty even when the marshal signaled them to close ranks. His absence was dramatic. Then the dean made the announcement followed by a silent prayer.

Louise set the table and brought in pork chops and vegetables. Elaine would forever remember some of the details of what followed: how the pork chops tasted like brown wrapping paper; how the combination of confusion and her desire to be alone found her standing up at the table, asking to be excused, in need of a hot bath; how the ancient iron bathtub with its claw feet welcomed and tried to soothe her; how she was stunned to notice that the water was becoming pink as she was still covered with so much dried blood. How, she wondered, could she still be breathing when her beloved Todd was dead? And then the tears, and the deeper release, and the sobbing so convulsive that it could soon be heard in the other room. Mother demanded to come into the bathroom but Uncle Robert intervened and insisted that she be left alone with this despair. She could not remember, later, how or when she fell asleep.

* * *

Elaine's disorientation upon awakening was frightening. She tried to make sense of this ceiling with its elaborate molding, this room with three different styles of lamps, this wall with its incongruous seascape painting, all so strange. But the voices in the other room were familiar: mother, Aunt Louise, Uncle Robert, Shirley. Figures from the worst nightmare now formed into the reality of yesterday. She measured the morning as Saturday. Sitting up in bed thrust her into sharp contact with the knifing pain of her hip, knee, elbow and shoulder. Then came the clear scene of her in the foyer, refusing to be dragged outdoors by the killer. And then the black steel of the gun butt, crashing down on her head, and the blood. Always the blood.

It was necessary to quiet her mind, to sit still for a minute, to focus on the new day, to reorient her body and summon it to work for her. Aunt Louise had left a robe and a hairbrush, the latter being useless because of the sutures in her scalp.

Again there was the unnatural silence as she entered the living room. Uncle Robert rose first and said: "I hope you slept deeply." She nodded. He pointed to the morning paper: "You are all over the news."

"She can read that later." Mother was again giving orders. "Have some breakfast. We will need to leave as soon as possible for Gary. I have called the funeral director. They will make all the arrangements when we get there."

The word was unreal, bizarre. Funeral. Funeral. She had never once thought about putting Todd's body in a box where everyone could come in a parade and look at him before they put him in the ground. To come look at Todd, to look at his smashed head and distorted face? A funeral for Todd? Todd who rubbed her feet, whose very life was kindness itself— dear Todd reduced to a corpse in a coffin? And her thoughts disappeared into a haze.

She said nothing and went to the kitchen, finding an empty seat at the table. Louise brought her toast and tea. Others were talking but she did not follow their trains of thought, as if their language were foreign. Louise offered her several options for clothing, all of which required some adjustments. She was dressing when she heard the knock at the door, and then recognized the voices of the detectives. Why were they here? Have they caught him? Or is it about Brian? She hurried out.

The tall detective greeted Elaine gently, asked her to be seated, and began his explanation. "We learned that you were going to Gary this morning and wanted to catch you before you left. Something has happened that we think you should know about."

An alarm began to clatter along her spine. The detective waited for her to be fully attentive.

"He came back last night to your house."

"What?"

"He came back to your place last night. We had a policewoman decoy there last night, just in case. She walked in front of the sheer drapes several times and, sure enough, he came to the window. Unfortunately when she went for him he got away."

There was a frozen silence. No one even moved.

"He thought he might catch you. That's why we had the decoy."

Muffled low sounds moved through the room. Uncle Robert walked over to stand close to Elaine, studying her face. It was a mask of stone.

The detective continued. "There's more. We have reason to believe he was in the hospital yesterday. Security noticed someone suspicious in the hallway, looking for someone. When security hailed him he ran."

Now the murmurs became expressions of bewilderment and fear. Mother stood and began to address the ineptitude of the police department for letting this animal get away. The detective ignored her, his eyes locked on Elaine. He interrupted Mother.

"Elaine, do you understand what we are saying?"

Her words were muted by her shallow breathing. "He came back? He actually returned to the house?"

"Don't you see? You and your brother are the only witnesses. With the two of you gone he thinks he would have nothing to worry about."

Now it was absolutely clear. He was not only out there, running free. He was not through with her. He wanted to come back and kill her.

The new awareness was that of being utterly hopeless. It was all but impossible to try to come to terms with the reality of yesterday, the horror behind her. But now there descended in her path a new terror which threatened to torture or destroy whatever future she might possibly have. This reality was all but unbearable: "He will always be out there looking for me."

"We had your house under surveillance last night and will continue to do so. We will have an undercover officer throughout the wake and funeral at Gary."

But his words trailed off. She could no longer hear him. With the past in ruin, the future an empty abyss, and with no escape from the present, she must disappear.

4. Transition

Brian's medical status was perplexing. His surgeon had made it clear that his condition was extremely critical and that if he did regain a semblance of consciousness, the family should not tell him about Todd's death as it would upset him. Yet when Elaine came to his bed on Tuesday he wept openly. He was intubated because of the lacerated lung, but around the tube he mouthed the words to her "I'm sorry. I'm so sorry."

He knew.

* * *

July 16, 1982

Elaine and Todd had periodically joked about the need of the other to see a shrink. It was usually a playful subject but sometimes one of great interest: a time someday to investigate one's own inner self.

But now it seemed to be something of an emergency. It was as if her psyche had undergone a kind of permanent anesthesia. Persons around her seemed unreal: bland faces without expression, voices echoing from far away, arms hanging strangely from their bodies. She felt numb, detached, watching herself go through blurred motions of the day. Her family was alarmed but that was of little concern to her. She had returned to her job at the medical school at Rush University Medical Center where her co-workers acted oddly toward her, sometimes attempting conversations that made no sense, other times seeming to avoid her. However, her obstetrician had insisted that she call this psychiatrist, a Dr. Richard Keith. And when she called Friday evening his response was immediate: "Can you see me Monday morning at 7:30?"

So now she was here, in his cozy office, interested to meet someone who might understand what she herself did not comprehend. At least on the phone he had sounded kind. She was relieved that he did not begin with paperwork as all the "clinicians" had done at the hospital. He sat, waiting; she sat, searching for a beginning. They studied each other for the early minute, she curling her feet under her in the cushy chair, he sitting back in his leather swivel, writing pad on the desk beside him. Finally:

"Dr. Freeman seemed to think it urgent that you come and see me. What do you think that is about?"

"Hmm. I am not sure. . . He seemed confused. . . Let's see. I guess mother called him first because I refused to take Imipramine. He said it would not affect my baby but I disagreed. Hmm . . . Then during the. . . the funeral, I began to cramp and was afraid of a miscarriage. I went to see him the next day and when he examined me he kept saying 'I don't believe you are pregnant.' I knew I was. He explained that my cervix did not indicate such. I insisted I was. I said 'I have to be pregnant. Otherwise I have no more reason to live.'"

"Can you say more about that?"

"It is obvious. I have nothing left. I need it to end. But I can't take the baby away from life. The baby is what remains of Todd."

* * *

July 16, 1982. Richard Keith, M.D. Intake dictation. Patient: Elaine Atkinson, DOB 07-25-58, referral by Carl Freeman, M.D. for suicidal ideation. 25 year-old female, average height and weight. Mental status deferred; only partial orientation to time, person, place and situation. Five weeks ago witnessed murder of her husband, attempted murder of her brother, herself physically assaulted. Requesting hospital records of her injuries.

Her narrative report of the trauma and subsequent events is often fragmented, disconnected. Claims she cannot remember salient details. Affect is flat with occasional congruence. Motivation for treatment apparently derives from being pregnant and protecting the infant. Lethality high.

* * *

July 19, 1982

"So doctor, the detectives came and took me back to the house this week. They wanted me to re-enact everything but I could remember so little. The house seemed somehow unfamiliar." A long pause. "One horrible thing. In the bedroom something smelled rotten. We looked around. Then I lifted up the water bed and there it was. The blood of my husband mixed with the washing water had run down the side to underneath the mattress. It was still there. Sickening. I told them to clean it up."

"How awful." Silence. "That's the first time you have been back in the house?"

She nods.

"Can you talk about what that was like, to go back in that front door, back into your living room. . . "

"I didn't want to be there. I wanted to help the detectives because they really want to catch the guy. They have asked me to look at so many mug shots. I guess it was necessary." Her speech is blunt, wooden.

"I would think being back there would trigger some memories of that night."

"Night. Morning." Silence.

"The rooms, the faces, the sounds . . . "

Although her face is tightly masked, her clutched hands and slight body tremors betray some inner convulsion. "What are you talking about? . . . Of course, Todd in bed. No... the sounds and the screaming. . . Brian on the floor. . . His face.

44

Dark face. He is out there now. . . Right now he is out there."
Her eyes dart around the room, over to the window.

Long silence. "It is hard for you to believe that you will
ever get him out of your mind or forget his face."

She nods, then curls up into the corner of her cushioned
chair, turns her head to her shoulder, and closes her eyes.

* * *

**July 20, 1982. Richard Keith, M.D., course of treatment
dictation. EA 07-25-58. Establishing rapport about which
she is understandably ambivalent. Symptoms: amnestic
spectrum, some lack of congruence in thoughts, anxiety
and depression, fitful sleep. Rejects all medication for
reasons of pregnancy. She appears basically functional
in the workplace which is non-relational and where she
manipulates electronic data. Living upstairs in home
of brother-in-law but prefers to be apart from others.
A number of interactions with police who speculate that
the killer picked her at random, perhaps following her late
husband home from his night visit to a doughnut shop.
Now it would appear that his single interest in her is to
eliminate her as a witness.**

* * *

Visiting Brian presented Elaine with a strange interlude
of peacefulness. It made no sense as he was in such pain,
and the doctors cautioned against premature assurance,
reminding everyone that he was "in a bad way with a long
way to go." But their grave words would only take her back
to the house and the flashing scenes of him on the floor,
bleeding, wheezing, at the edge of death. So, in spite of it
all, she believed that he would recover. He would remain

indefinitely in intensive care. But he must recover. He was the incarnation of hope: strong and young, and she found courage in holding his hand, a fellow survivor. Even if his was the only hand in the world.

* * *

July 23, 1982

"You seem to have more energy, more focus when you are talking about meeting with the police."

"Yeah. . . Yeah, they seem confident, tough." A slight smile. "He is not going to mess with them. And they want him bad. . . I guess all the fingerprints were too smeared. They said the gun was a 45 caliber. Five shots had been fired. And he would have killed me too except he ran out of bullets. . . Makes them wonder if he had used those bullets earlier in the evening." Long silence. "They had me look at all those mug shots again, and on Friday I went to a line-up. Six of them."

"No luck?"

A long sigh. "One of them seemed familiar: height, skin, size of his head. But I couldn't be sure. You see, all of them in the lineup were acting cocky, joking, smug. The face I know was fierce and hateful." She turned to look out the window. "How will I ever find that face before it finds me?"

A lengthy silence follows. Finally he spoke: "Where did you just go?"

Rising from her chair, Elaine goes over to the window, looking away. A long pause. "I don't really know. . . Thinking of his face, my mind goes off into the streets of the city, into some room where he is sitting right now. Right this minute. . . That creates some kind of. . . some kind of a connection and I am pulled out of myself somehow. . . Ah, I know I am in this chair, but this other part of me is lost out there somewhere."

"This other part of you . . ."

"Yeah. My, my . . . what used to be myself."

"And if you try to call your "self" back to you, to join with you here . . ."

"It usually doesn't work. . . She won't come back. . . It is not safe here, with me. If he finds me, he gets her. . . Hmm. Well, she comes back sometimes. She joins me again when I stand beside Brian at the hospital."

"Any idea why that happens?"

Returning to her chair. "Brian and I are safe together. We have been through it. If we are back to back, no one can slip up behind us."

A long silence. "You say you can remember almost nothing of Todd's funeral. The thought just came to me, that if Brian had been there with you it might have been safe enough for your "self" to join you."

She nods, but it is difficult to interpret.

Another minute or two. She looks up. "You talk about "the two of me." Are you suggesting that I am schizophrenic or something?"

"Oh no. Not that. You are not psychotic. But there is a serious splitting here. I guess it is the only way you have found to cope with something so overwhelming . . . so vast that you are doing the best you can. We call it dissociating, removing yourself. You put it well: you let your "self"' go far from you."

"Yeah. I seem to be a magnet for disaster." Looking him in the eye. "Best to stay away from me."

"But with Brian you bring it back together."

"Sure. He went through it with me."

"So . . . give some thought to how we might make that happen in this office."

"What?"

"You. You being here together. Here, working with me."

* * *

July 25, 1982. Richard Keith, M.D. Course of treatment dictation. EA 07-25-58. Severe symptoms. Patient feeling permanently damaged. Estrangement from herself is expressed in a literal dissociation with self. Social withdrawal except from brother and from police whom she considers advocates and her one hope of finding the killer. Brother's recovery vital for her. Otherwise detached, mechanical at work, all other interests diminished. Ongoing dissociative state with amnesia.

* * *

Brian was very alert and focused. His speech was labored because of the intubation, but he eagerly worked around it. He found being with Elaine a blessed respite from his physical misery. With her he felt safe, free to weep, free to smile or tell an ironic joke. Todd was dead; he was alive; she was alive; some kind of future beckoned, whether that would be a rebirth or a curse.

"You didn't want to come to the graduation. You told me about your premonition. You must be thinking that you should have trusted that and stayed in Detroit."

He immediately shook his head. "No. No! I fought the trip over. But I also had the strongest certainty that if I did not come worse things would have happened." He has to stop and cadence his breath. "And that is true. If I had not come you would have died."

Elaine had no response. This safe place was suddenly becoming complicated with paradoxes and mysteries which taxed her.

"But let me tell you something else. Something happened that was even worse than being shot."

Elaine turned to him, not understanding a word he was saying. "What could ever be worse?"

"I was awake during surgery."

"What are you saying?"

"The anesthesia was what they called "light." Apparently with my loss of blood, the nick in my heart, and everything else, if I went too "deep" I might not have survived." A long pause to catch his breath. "That was worse than the gun. I was paralyzed but awake. I underwent an actual vivisection. Stuff you have read about in science fiction."

A careful pause. "Brian, we have been through hell. How can you know what is real and what is not?"

"Find the team that was in surgery. I can tell you what was said. They split me from stem to stern. Then for the lung, a lateral cut around from the spine to my gut. I haven't seen it yet but that is what is there."

Elaine changed the subject. This was macabre, the last thing she needed to hear. Brian was delusional; she was delusional, nothing was what it seemed to be.

Two days later when she visited him Brian was feisty. "Go ahead. Talk to the staff. Their faces went white, their eyes wide, as I repeated things that were said during my surgery. When they told the anesthesiologist, they said he was defensive, dismissing me as out of my mind. Yet they noted that he agreed to change the medical record to report that the patient said that he approached consciousness twice during the surgical procedure as a result of anesthetic precautions."

* * *

July 31, 1982

"Sorry I am late. Can't seem to help it. Everything is just all strung out." She moves first from the office chair, then to the sofa where she lies down.

After a pause. "You are finding it difficult to just get here."

Irritably. "I am not even at home in my own skin. It has been this way all week."

"Tell me about that."

"Where to begin? . . . You know I told you that I had to move upstairs into the apartment on the third floor. I just didn't feel safe on the first floor, even living with Todd's family. . . I mean Dave's name is in the phone book and he was mentioned in the newspaper. I could be tracked down. . . . However, now Barbara, my sister-in-law, sometimes comes up to my place when I am gone. She's not being snoopy. It's okay that she has a key, if she just wants to borrow ketchup or something. But I will see signs of it instantly when I get home. Maybe a shoe has been moved one inch, and I will notice it. It gets real freaky. Then I look in the closets and under the bed."

"Sure."

"But that is nothing compared to the other night. Just after midnight I heard this sharp, cracking sound. I was awake in a second but could not move. I listened and listened, trying to hear what came next. I wondered if it was Misty, our cat. But I knew it was not. I was frozen, the worse panic I can ever remember. My breathing came in short gasps, like I was sobbing. But I was afraid to make a sound, even to take a deep breath . . .afraid that he would hear me and know where I was. . .wondering why he was waiting so long.. . wondering what I could do if I saw him first. . . This went on for what seemed like an hour. I kept thinking 'I am on the third floor and no one can climb up.' Finally I managed to get up and turn on one light. And there it was: a curtain rod had fallen down. That's all. But it was horrible."

"That kind of panic is truly horrible. You try to face reality and to know that you are safe on the third floor, but the sound, the return to all the fears. . . "

"I didn't know how to cope with it. I don't know how to do this."

"How did you get through the rest of the night?"

"I kept rubbing my stomach. I focused on the baby inside of me. Safely within me. There is the reason to hang on. I just closed out everything else and imagined a future when I would be with a baby who would be smiling at the mobiles above her bassinet, and splashing in her little bath, or cooing. And I would be smiling again."

* * *

July 31, 1982. Richard Keith, M.D. Course of treatment dictation. EA 07-25-58. Severe anxiety leading to hyper-vigilance and panic states. Treatment complicated by her aversion to any medication. Working DX: Post Traumatic Stress Syndrome, Severe, which subsumes integral features of dissociative and amnestic states, social withdrawal, depersonalization and de-realization. Her pregnancy provides a vital grounding in reality.

* * *

Brian was in ICU for almost a month, most of the time intubated. But he did rally and when the time came for his release, Sharon arrived from Detroit to accompany him back. His near death restored their connection, but as he was recuperating at home it became apparent that old dysfunctional patterns were re-appearing and they both began to know it could not last.

Elaine was surprised at how much she missed Brian's presence. Dr. Keith reminded her that Brian was the only other person, beside himself, that she really made contact with, and then he reminded her that, unlike her relationship with Brian, she was very selective with what she would discuss in therapy.

And it was true. Elaine would talk with Brian by phone two or three times a week. They were mutual survivors, both trying to get back but knowing it would never be to the life they had known.

On one late evening, Elaine's anxiety was a riptide of cross currents pulling her away from her anchors to a place beyond all safety. She fought it, pacing the floor, turning on music that she thought would soothe, then turning that off. She tried to meditate but was unable to find even a momentary haven. She finally called Brian who tried to get her to focus. At last she found herself speaking of the turbulence at her core. "I think this baby is going to die, and that will be the end of it for me."

Brian's response was consistent with the rawness of his life. "You mean you would commit suicide?"

"Yeah. There would be nothing left. But then maybe there is nothing left anyway. Sometimes I also think that if the baby lives I will give it up for adoption and then suicide. Then this will be over."

"Have you talked about this with your doctor?"

"Oh no."

"Why not?"

"He would just try to talk me out of it. That's his job."

* * *

August 13, 1982

"I just had to quit my job at Rush. It had become too awkward. I tried to avoid the other workers, just wanting to focus on my work. But I couldn't concentrate. I could only think about this baby. Or I would suddenly be reminded about the killer out there. He might find out I worked there. That thought would trigger a new round of panic, and then I would wonder if I was hurting the baby."

Dr. Keith finally breaks the silence. "Have you told your obstetrician of your frustrations, your difficulties."

"No, he is rather glib. He is well accustomed to pregnant women being occasionally queasy. He always, always just reassures me: 'No need to worry. Everything is going to be just fine.' But I suppose now you will call and tell him that that I am critical."

"No Elaine, I don't work that way. Or maybe you are still having trouble deciding how much you can trust me, or our working together."

A long pause. She looks at him directly, then finally turns away. "No, we are doing okay. I think maybe it is Dr. Freeman's office. Are you aware I can look out of his window and see my old house. Just three blocks away. And I look at it, and look at it, and nothing could be more familiar, but also nothing could be more alien. Right there but in another world."

"Right there is the place, but it is like it is not in this world." Another long pause. "Keep talking about that. You have been reluctant, or unable these months to recall all that happened at that place."

Quickly. "I have gone through all of that with the cops. I don't need any more of it. Every time they call me in to look at pictures I am back there again."

"Have they shown you pictures of the . . . the murder scene?"

Closing her eyes. "They don't need to. They are in my head."

"All of them?"

With heightened tension: "No."

"So you look out the window at Dr. Freeman's, and there it is, and you keep looking even though you want to look away . . . "

"Yeah. Damned if I do and damned if I don't. . . . Damned I guess."

Pause. "Damned if you see it all because all the horror returns and damned if you look away because. . . well, how is it damning if you don't look at it? What's that like for you?"

Elaine rises from her chair, walks to the window, her hands cupping the sides of her head, close to tears. "What's it like? Like a part of me is not connected, unattached, just drifting away."

"That's got to be a terrible impasse."

She returns to her chair, sits back, and speaks mechanically. "Let's talk about this baby in here. That is very real."

* * *

August 23, 1982. Richard Keith, M.D. Dictating quarterly summary course of treatment. EA 07-25-58. Post Traumatic Syndrome, Severe. Periodic, even predictable, episodes of

dissociation, de-realization. She appears to swing between two strategies of coping. On the one hand her analytic mind wants to understand what is happening to her, how to explain her frequent sense of not even being in her own skin. When she is in this mode she seems to be motivated for psychotherapy, truly desiring to probe her lost memories. Then she will swing to a position of repression, welcoming the ability to just block out the trauma. When she is in this mode she is distant from me, minimizing any importance to our contact, wanting to talk only of how to cope with her pregnancy.

Her brother, Brian, returned to Detroit for recovery from his critical wounds. She was very upset by his apparently credible report that he was partially conscious during his own surgery. She was confused, both angry and empathetic, that he described the surgical trauma as even worse than the murder scene at her home. She talks with him regularly as she has no other social contacts.

The course of therapy should persist with its focus on optimal support while at the same time attempting to facilitate her recovery of memory, at least enough memory to reduce the dissociative episodes and eliminate de-realization swings.

I watch the developments of her pregnancy very carefully. It is troubling that the child she bears is experienced as her only reason for living. I would guess that she has discussed suicidal thoughts with her brother but has resisted the subject in her therapy.

* * *

September 10, 1982

As Elaine paces the floor by the office window, she mutters: "I was so hopeful that my new job at the bookstore would work out. However, I'm just furious at my boss. What a neolith! Paleolith!"

After a moment Dr. Keith responds, wryly: "Your boss. . . he dresses in animal skins and carries a club?"

"Ha! That would be easy. No, he is just a thinking machine with no understanding of humans. No feelings. He makes Mr. Spock on Star Trek look like Mother Theresa."

"What happened to spark this fire in you?"

"He is just so insensitive. For weeks he has frowned, been short, been impatient. But this week it all came out. He looked at me and actually said 'You should be over this by now. It has been over three months. Life goes on.'"

A huge sigh. "Incredible."

"Short of getting a shotgun and going out and shooting every suspicious man I see, what constitutes 'getting over it'?"

Quietly, after a very long pause. "Stay with this. All those feelings. . ."

"No, I think if I do I will explode."

"This is the safest place in town to explode."

Elaine turns, scrutinizing his face, especially his eyes, and his posture. There is reassurance in his underlying confidence. Or is he really so confident? Is this some kind of routine, some drill he was taught to manage people like her? She then sits down, takes a sip of water, looks to the ceiling and sighs.

"Well, how do people 'get through' things like this? How do they, as they glibly say, 'move on'?"

"We can't generalize about all people. Our focus is just on you."

"So am I making progress or not?"

"What do you think?"

"Progress. Hmm. That is a hollow word. An illusion."

"Maybe. . . can you imagine . . . can you depict a scene in the future where you are moving into a new chapter of your life, and all of this . . . "

"Is far behind me? Forgotten? You've got to be kidding."

"Of course not forgotten. How could you forget? But maybe worked through in such a way that you were free of the hold it had on you."

"I don't understand. Hold on me?"

Thoughtfully. "That the time might come when all of your energy was not devoted to this struggle, when you could remember whatever you needed to remember, but you were now free to think and feel about other things."

"Like my baby?"

"Sure. A new chapter."

"No, the baby will forever remind me of Todd. He lives in the baby. This will go on forever."

"Not if you try to deal with life as it goes on."

"You are not very clear today. What are you talking about? 'Life as it goes on.'"

"It is like some core part of your life just stopped when Todd was killed. Oh, you will talk with the cops, come here, go to work, and go to your obstetrician. But in your own words your 'self' gets disconnected from you here. Often she is out there somewhere, looking for the killer I guess. I wish she would join us here."

"To do what?"

"To start dealing with the real life that followed Todd's death."

"The 'real life'?"

"Yes. Elaine, are you aware that you have not talked about the funeral, the cemetery, your family, what people did and said. . . you know, the real life that continued."

"I can't remember."

"I don't buy that. The truth is that those memories are so painful that you muster all your strength to shut them off, to bury them."

"So."

"So what is the consequence? The result is that you and your "self" do not come together and go forward. You are trapped in a world of what used to be."

A long pause. "Do you really think I can recover those memories? Hmm. And do you really think I should?"

"I think you are ready to open many of them. Maybe not all. You are free to repress certain things. We all do. But the more you repress, the more you are imprisoned. The very walls that keep the bad things out are the walls that lock you in."

Another long pause. Finally, she rises from the chair. "Our time is about up."

"That's usually my line. Yes, let's pick up here next time."

* * *

"September 17, 1982

"I'm telling you, I just don't remember very much. I don't think I am 'psychologically repressing' as you say. I was just too distracted. No memories."

"Do you have early childhood memories?"

"Like what?"

"Oh, your first day of school. Or your favorite Christmas present. Or your first airplane trip?"

"Well sure. We all have memories. What is your point?"

"Those important things are recorded for us to recall, or revisit. Especially things that are powerful. And I can't imagine anything more powerful than that night/morning at your house."

"And you think it is necessary for me to go revisit that, to remember it all? Why should I want to do that?"

"Of course you don't want to do that. It is painful. And I am not even pushing you to remember all the details so much as I want for you to claim your range of feelings about that time, to keep being reminded of how much psychic energy you are using to wall them off. It even splits you apart."

A long pause. Finally: "I want to get up and leave right now . . . But then I do ask myself, what is the risk of remembering? What is the risk?"

"Stay with that question."

Eyes closed, head back on the pillow. "All I knew is that I was alive. I know we are all going to die sometime. But that is somewhat philosophical. What happened is that my life could have ended right then. But it didn't. I was alive. And Todd was not. And Brian might not make it. I was alive and glad I was alive, then I hated that I was alive. And I hated that bastard alive out there and ready to make other people dead."

"'Glad I was alive, and hated that I was alive.' Those are really powerful feelings to claim."

Long pause. "Yeah, I can have sharp memories of that room, that moment. But why have I just kind of erased the days that followed?"

"Why do you think?"

"Hmm. I guess the full reality of it hit me. . . Todd there in the coffin . . . All of those people. . . What some of them did and said. . . "

"See if you can tell me about some of that."

"I don't even know where to pick it up."

"Here, lie back on the sofa. Close your eyes if you want. No particular order here. If a memory bubbles up, claim it and your feelings about it."

She moves to the sofa and lies down. "Where did we last leave off that story?"

"I think you were at your uncle's house on a Saturday, and were going back to Gary to make arrangements."

"Oh that trip. I don't remember even who was in the car. Just blurred. Someone mentioned funeral and I felt unreal. 'Funeral.' A gross word. . .Mother, of course. . . Mother, always so logical. Mother had called some 'funeral' home she knew about. . . . Maybe she knew them through her church. . . Oh yeah, that funeral director was a young guy, and his wife was pregnant. . . I don't know where Todd was just then. . ."

"Take your time."

"Hmm. . . I picked out the casket. I insisted on making that choice. It had a blue lining. Yes, a golden oak casket with a blue satin lining. He would look good in his blue graduation suit, and the new blue shirt I bought for him . . ." Long, long pause. "I did not want Todd embalmed, just buried. But some stupid law requires it." Longer pause. "Now what?"

"Just free associate, that is, let yourself respond to whatever it is you remember."

"Let's see. . . I was driven away somewhere, then back again. Late that afternoon, I guess. Before what they strangely called 'visiting hours.' Yes, yes. Todd was there in that blue-lined coffin. I moved to him, ran my hands over him. . . He felt so cold, so stiff. It didn't look quite like him. I remember observing that it was amazing they could put him together at all. I felt his hair and the bullet hole they sutured up. . . I just petted him, put my head on his chest, and cried and cried and cried. . . He was so cold. . . Suddenly the whole family was there, his family and mine. The funeral director asked them to stand back while I had . . . solitary contact. . . But they just watched me, and then he and I were not alone. Then all of those people, a circus. Oh yes, those two women. I was holding Todd's hand talking to his sister when I overheard this one woman say to the other 'I don't see a bullet hole. I thought he was shot in the head.' I wanted to choke her. . . . I don't remember the rest of the evening."

"What then?"

"The funeral at mother's church. Very vague . . . recorded music, old traditional church hymns . . . Mother's pastor preached. . . I do recall that he made no mention that the deceased had a widow. Todd's mother was crying and made that comment 'three people there, and why did it have to be Todd?' My immediate thought was 'I would have preferred to die, not Todd, but Todd would have wanted his baby to live and not die with me.' Did I hear that or imagine it? . . . No, I heard it. . . Also at the funeral Todd's father sobbing and Todd's mother telling him 'Stop. You are making a fool of yourself. We should all be happy Todd is now in heaven.' And I said it so she could hear me 'I would rather have him here.'" Quiet, soft tears.

"You have never talked about any of this to anyone?"

"No." Pause. "And the rest I don't really remember. They say there were over three hundred people there. But I just took myself away. I know how to do that."

"You know how to . . . to take yourself away?"

"It is what you might call a self-hypnotic thing. I look for some little opening, some crack in space or creation, something moving or sparkling or beautiful, and just disappear into it."

"How did this happen at the funeral?"

"I do remember the stained glass up high, toward the ceiling, and the beams of light being refracted through the various shades of blue. The beautiful stained glass filled with the sun. The ribbons of blues, interwoven, moving into soft swirls, into a distant blue fog. They were rhythmic, dancing into a helix, and turned to me and beckoned, welcomed me to leave that place. To follow them through this realm into another. And I did. So I really don't have any further memories. I had disappeared."

"You talk about this so naturally, with such familiarity. With such confidence."

"I learned it when I was young. The way to survive at home. I think I had to turn to it briefly at the hospital, too. I remember starting to disappear down a river when the nurses came and pulled me back. Against my will."

"That seems to be a very important function of your central self. I hope you can teach me more about that."

Pause. "Maybe. . . But not now. And I really think those are all the memories I have of that . . . that funeral."

＊　＊　＊

November 3, 1982. Richard Keith, M.D. Dictating quarterly summary of treatment. EA 07-25-58. Post Traumatic Stress Syndrome, severe. Some progress on contact and engagement with the patient. Some memory recall, but the problem is not so much that of amnesia as it is of how she has learned to dissociate during extreme crisis. Some memories may not be available to her as she disconnected from the reality of the traumatic moment. She apparently learned what she describes as a "self-hypnotic" procedure during which times she experiences part of her affective self as actually "disappearing." I am challenging her at this juncture: while honoring this defense as a strategic coping mechanism, I am calling on her to recognize how dysfunctional it is for her. During these times she is affectively flat or even void while remaining cognitively adequate. The work will be to rebuild self-support in a manner where she can re-integrate these "two sides" of her personality functioning.

I am also concerned about this last trimester of her pregnancy. She frequently frets about the fetus, fearing it will die in-utero or at birth. This anxiety is excessive and troublesome in that she concludes that this would end her reason for living. I examine this closely as a possible justification for her own underlying suicidal impulses, or more deeply held homicidal impulses.

* * *

November 12, 1982.

"Sometimes you are as blasé as my obstetrician."

"How is that?"

"I am not getting any bigger. . . Sometimes the baby does not move inside for long periods of time. I go to my O.B. almost weekly now. He just reassures me in his well-practiced style. 'Be happy, the baby is moving, everything is fine.' Yeah. Just because the baby is moving does not mean everything is fine."

"Of course you are anxious . . ."

"No, you think I am just one more fussy-mother-to-be. No, this is very intense. I have a connection with this baby. This is Todd living in me. Here is my reason for hanging on. When I feel signs of life I can actually foresee a future when life resumes and goes on. I can push on through this exhaustion and the queasiness. But then . . . "

"But then . . . "

61

A long pause. Finally, a deep sigh, a shift in her chair, a remote stare out of the window. "Never mind."

"Stay with what you were thinking. . . what you were going to say."

Extended silence. "Elaine, you just stopped right in the middle of something important, some genuine thought or feeling. Maybe something very frightening."

Mechanically. "Well, so?"

Pause. "So you came to that intersection and something, whatever it was, was so real that you dealt with it in . . . what? . . . in this kind of resignation, this stoic indifference."

"Sure. . . "

Extended silence. "Let me ask you. Have you prepared for a nursery at home? Have you gone shopping for the clothes, diapers, supplies . . . "

"Why go shopping if there is no baby."

"Elaine, look at me. Mental health is facing reality, life the way it really is rather than what someone says it should be, or shouldn't be. So in reality there has been no medical reason to believe that there is anything wrong with your baby."

"You don't understand either. I am pretty sure this baby is going to die, and then that will be the end of it."

* * *

Elaine kept remembering how, as a child, the time between Thanksgiving and Christmas seemed like forever. And she had reason for that association this December: just as the Christmas tree used to be tantalizing, promising surprises that it seemed were never going to be forthcoming, so now the little bassinet in the nursery beckoned to her, almost mocking her. It was like a sad fairy tale in the making.

And another beckoning occurred on her weekly trip to her obstetrician's office. She now deliberately avoided being near the window from which she could immediately see the old house. The place where this baby was conceived was the same place where this baby's father was destroyed. And when she looked at the house her eyes would lift to search the city beyond, out there where he was. Yet the energy that was required to resist the invitation of the window only added to her exhaustion.

She again complained to her doctor that her stomach still seemed way too small, but he merely moved the projected date of birth further down on the calendar. There would be occasional movement followed by haunting stretches of empty time. He did suggest that she begin Lamaze training, and when she mentioned this to Brian he immediately offered to be her coach. Yet this, too, troubled her. Brian's negative perspective on life was increasing, and she imagined if something went wrong he would simply accept it stoically and cynically. So he would not do. Instead, she would ask the Lamaze instructor for the name of a suitable coach.

Her avoidance of people provided her with a quiet refuge, but the cost was high as she was intensely aware of being almost totally alone. She was accustomed to her family having contact with her only out of their morbid curiosity. She would sometimes converse with Dave and Barbara downstairs but no one else. She would use her voice when talking on the phone to Brian, but otherwise silence prevailed. Just she and Misty the cat, the two post-traumatic stress victims. Ever since the night of the murder, Misty would hide at the sound of a man's voice. And Elaine felt this fear in common with her cat. Even at the market she observed that she made no eye contact with clerks or cashiers. They apparently were familiar with recluses like her and respected her space. She had always been an extrovert, socially gregarious, even the life of some parties in not so distant times. But now as she sat in the utter quietness, she was continuously aware of a baby within her, a baby sometimes alarmingly inactive – and also continuously aware that, outside in that city, he was there, and he could become very active.

* * *

Christmas came and went without notice and with no Christmas tree. Brian had called and they talked for an hour. He was predictably jaundiced about the holiday season. Elaine vented her frustrations with the obstetrician who kept moving back the date of delivery. She noted that by one of the doctor's calculations Todd could not possibly be the father. Then she would return to her own chronic queasiness and the baby's lack of movement. She reported an ultrasound which detected a possible lesion on her placenta.

But in January events began to quickly unfold. During one stress test, there were no fetal reactions. Elaine did not sleep that night. The next day amniotic fluid was drawn with alarming results: the yield was a green fluid, a sign that the fetus had a bowel movement. Her doctor told her "You are going to have to deliver this baby today or tomorrow. Get in touch with your Lamaze teacher." But the nurse who ran the Lamaze class gave an immediate and adamant response to the doctor: "Do it now!"

As they prepped her, Elaine asked for a mirror to be placed so she could watch the birth. It turned out that this was not a completely uncommon request and they brought in a pedestal with a tall stand and a gooseneck for the mirror, up above the medical personnel. The conversation focused quickly on her increasing nausea, a determination that she was ten weeks premature, a concern that the baby might not survive labor. As she watched the process her thoughts went momentarily to Brian's report of being awake during his radical surgery, what he referred to as an actual vivisection. That association provoked such a powerful wave of anxiety that it was immediately noticed by the team, and the nurse held her hands and guided her deep breathing.

But finally through her tears Elaine watched in the mirror as a tiny blue baby emerged. And it was moving! A nurse said, calmly, "You have a baby girl." When they presented her, Elaine cried. A sweet, wrinkled little thing, white on her nose, brown fuzzy ears, looking up at her mother through squinting eyes. She weighed three pounds, fourteen ounces. They said her APGAR scores were adequate. And Elaine gave the doctor the name by which she would be called in her new life: Ellen Atkinson.

And later, as the orderly was taking Elaine and Ellen to their private room, she was met in the hall by a man in a white coat with a dear smile. It was Dr. Richard Keith. He took her hand and said that he just wanted to be there.

* * *

The baby was lethargic and would not easily feed. In Neo-Natal Intensive Care she was initially placed on IV's, then fed one ounce and a half every hour, roughly twenty times in a twenty-four hour period. Throughout the first week, Elaine held her daughter whenever she could, but quietly reflected on how she was having a difficult time feeling attached or bonded. She brooded on the doctor's false prediction that the baby would be around five pounds at birth, and began to passively accept a reality where the baby would die. But on the other hand, when she overheard the medical staff discussing Ellen's status, and when one suggested that perhaps the baby was a victim of congenital toxoplasmosis, which would fatally calcify the brain, Elaine was angry, loud, challenging them all: "This baby is fine. Don't you dare say that there is something wrong with her." That evening she imagined that she was sorting this confusion out in therapy. First distance from the child, then total alliance. And there came a clear insight: she was quite naturally defending herself against another possible loss, and would counter any resignation with fierce determination.

The child rallied against odds. One doctor told her "This baby is lucky to be alive. Born any earlier or any later and she would not have been able to handle it." But she prevailed, pink of cheek and with a new weight of four pounds, five ounces, she was released to go home.

Leaving the hospital was a rushed and disorganized affair with Dave carrying the baby to the car and Barbara loading all the clothes and supplies. But the baby just slept through the jumbled transition. And so, suddenly, Elaine was upstairs, for the first time truly alone with Ellen. And in the stillness her little eyes opened, searching, following signals of light and movement. And then an incredible focus: looking up at her mother, appearing to study the one holding her. Elaine was motionless, fixed upon that little face, the tiny wet lips, the wisp of hair, and transfixed by those eyes. If Ellen's little brain was taking it all in and working through her primal orientation as to how it all works, so Elaine found that her own mind was too small to comprehend the wonder of the moment. For a very long moment they looked into each other's eyes. Then two little waving hands appeared, one finding its own mouth.

The nursing took up most of an hour, time for Ellen to contemplate the essential meaning of the word miracle. For this was miracle itself. That this beautiful child was delivered whole and aware. That both were alive and now connected in love and determination for a new life. Was there a song that addressed such a moment? She tried to compose, but there were no words adequate. Only the humming sound of the most intimate joy.

But so soon the old familiar pack of challenges returned. Life began to consist of endless feeding and changes of diapers. And in the quietness, she stared outside of her winter windows at the monotony of the harsh chalk landscape, the daily snows crusting with soot and dirt. She tried to image times now past and would close her eyes to try to catch the ancient echo of horses clopping down the street. But the present was a world of shadows, empty skies devoid of birds, skeletal limbs of trees offering no promise of ever again shining with green.

She reflected on her solitude. Dr. Keith kept suggesting this withdrawal was pathological, or at least, as he said, "reinforced her apartness from real life." Yes. But maybe it was solace. Necessary even. She began to think of the monasteries, or the long list of spiritual leaders who had to go into the desert. For what? For healing? The desert outside her window was composed not of sand but of the constant cold grey skies of Chicago in February and the weekly snows off Lake Michigan. Distant traffic moved slowly, windows frosted as temperatures dropped, and the winds would gust without warning, growling and sometimes thrashing the third floor of her apartment building. This was her desert. Occasionally she had to venture out to the doctor or to the store, patiently bundling Ellen for the trip, sometimes being scolded by strangers for having a baby out in such frigid conditions. Then she would return to her hermitage where one day passed only to be followed by another of the same, February turning into March.

There were occasional interruptions which she privately welcomed. She had taken up sewing for Ellen, and when an old college roommate came by with preemie infant clothes Elaine was delighted. "Now she actually looks like a baby" she said. Another time two old friends from school dropped in to suggest that she needed to join them at a movie. They had a baby-sitter in mind, but Elaine would not possibly agree.

In their seclusion, Elaine studied Ellen at length, and the resemblance to Todd began to emerge, more focused with each new day. This only amplified her pervasive sadness. Todd would never see his baby nor would Ellen ever see her father. He would never watch her sleep, comb her hair, be enchanted by these first smiles, adore her sounds; and Ellen would never feel his strength or know his sound and smell. Never. In March she called Dr. Keith and resumed her work, this time with the baby in arms. He was very supportive, and sometimes she could glimpse a wave of pain across his face as she referred to the "empty plate at our table." But he was reassuring and she seemed to gain confidence. Once he even said to her "Maybe you don't need a psychotherapist any more, just people to talk to." And she replied "No, I always have to take care of people I talk to. I don't have to take care of you."

It was then that the life insurance check came and events were set in motion that would activate all the family and permanently disrupt the solitude. Dave and Barbara, downstairs, were first to notice the check when it came in the mail, and responded "What a wonderful thing!" To which Elaine immediately replied: "What a terrible price to pay." Elaine could not bring herself to cash the check for a month. But finally she did, motivated by the need to forward funds to Brian who was in difficult straits in his recovery.

But the word was out. Dave and Barbara made the initial overture. They were in trouble with the IRS and now had a solution. Elaine would buy them a house on the shores of Lake Michigan which they had found. They would pay her back, over time, in monthly rent. And the house had a nice room for Elaine and the baby.

Elaine finessed the house on Lake Michigan "offer" as best she could. Then came a call from sister Sarah. She and her husband needed to replace their car. Then Shirley requested funds for her children's clothing and, of course, mother got word and presented her case for a new carpet. And now Dave and Barbara, just downstairs, were incensed that their need was not being given priority.

* * *

March 17, 1983

Ellen sat in quiet wonder on her mother's lap, her wide eyes studying the man sitting in the chair and scanning the room with its blend of lights and color. This was another new place in a new day in a new life. It was a soft moment, in contrast to the sharp edge of mother's voice.

"Everyone is pissed off because of the money. As always I feel responsible for them."

"I hope you can just keep reminding yourself of what Todd bought the life insurance for. He made the investment for you and your daughter. He wanted to take care of you."

Long silence. Soft tears. "You are right. Most of my consciousness of Todd just deepens my sadness. But to think of him as seeing the insurance agent to protect me, that grounds me. He would not mind my helping Brian. . . who was there."

A long pause. "Think out loud."

"I just. . . how to even get my head around my crazy family. . . Do you know what my mother said? She was going on and on about being so depressed over not having a new carpet, and then she commented 'If I had a gun I would just shoot myself.' . . . Many of them have always been casual, glib about suicide."

After another long pause. "You were not casual or glib last year about your suicidal thoughts."

Restless, searching for words, then looking him in the eye. "No. As a matter of fact, I understated it to you. I would, most certainly, have killed myself after Todd was murdered if I had not been pregnant. You knew that. But you did not know how frequently the idea of that solution remained with me. In fact, several times I came to the firm decision that when the baby was born I would arrange for her to be adopted out. Then I would be free to end it all."

"Adoption and then suicide. . . . You never mentioned harboring those plans."

"No, I thought you would be required to stop me."

"And could I have stopped you?"

"Of course not. Temporarily, but not when I am off alone."

"What made you change your mind?"

"I haven't yet . . . Oh, I have. This little face. . . that smile when I sing to her. . . the way she grows silent when she puts her head on my chest and senses my heart beating. (Holding Ellen close to her.) She needs me, really needs me. So unlike my family. . . You see, well, in my family you grow up with the notion of suicide as a rather natural thing."

* * *

Slowly March evolved and the days began to lengthen. The advent of springtime was on the minds of newscasters and promised by the early garden displays in stores. But spring was not literally in the air when the winds brought a frigid blast, bringing still another major storm to the snow belt along Lake Michigan. It was a stubborn winter, one demanding respect, and it did not begin to yield until April arrived. And finally the sun broke through, as did the cautious crocus and daffodils, and the birds returned with morning song, and the neighborhood blossomed with forsythia and redbud. Elaine opened her window to the new season, encouraged by the proud tulips in the garden below, by the dogs on leashes alive and eager to explore the winter humus beyond the bushes just out of their reach. By mid-April the warmth was genuine and she could take Ellen out in a stroller for her first glimpse of all the activity in her first springtime. She purchased window boxes and planted small flowers. Sleep was more gentle and mornings more welcome. In her therapy she reflected on the first genuine sense of promise she had known since the disaster, and, at Easter, her own kind of resurrection: she and Ellen and the start of a new chapter of life.

The new routines were stabilizing for her. Strolling with the baby was carefully planned for each day in May. Housecleaning and shopping were scheduled, plants watered, calls with Brian expected. She returned to her reading, to select television shows, and always, always just sitting and watching her daughter grow.

Then came the day it happened, the devastating collapse of her newly reconstructed world. While casually scanning the morning paper, Elaine was instantly stricken. There, announced by a loud headline, was the prominent story about Todd's murder. "It has been exactly a year since the young dentist was killed in front of his wife. The case is still unsolved; the killer still not known. There is a reward for any information. . ."

She was in shock. Her breathing had all but stopped, her vision blurred. But she felt compelled to read further and there it was, reference to the widow who now had a baby to raise by herself.

Elaine, instantly nauseous, rushed to the bathroom and threw up. Trembling violently, she felt absolutely vulnerable – and then furious. Reporters had never asked her permission about this story, had not even tried to contact her. This was, for them, just good copy, a crime-stopper appeal.

She found it difficult to focus, to know what to do. She closed the window, shut the blinds, picked up Ellen, and huddled into the rocker. She had given no thought to the "anniversary" of the murder. And now this announcement for the public to observe the memory of a year ago. A year ago. A day like today only a year ago. That reality began to unfold, a year ago now intruding into this day. June 12. June 12. Todd and Brian asleep when she heard the sound. The gun with the man. The explosions. Brian gasping for air. Todd's brain matter on the rug. Being dragged by her hair. Gun to her head but misfiring.

Enough. Enough. You must always put it away.

She held sleeping Ellen closely. She did not know, simply did not know what to do. She thought of calling Brian, or calling Dr. Keith, or calling the newspaper reporter. But to say what? To expect what?

In the very act of staring at the phone, considering making a call, it rang. She was startled, thinking perhaps Brian or Dr. Keith had read her mind somehow. She picked up the receiver.

"Hello?"

A deep voice. "Hello. Do you remember me?"

Frozen. "Who is this?"

"Don't you recognize my voice? I'll bet you remember me."

Shouting. "Who is this?"

"You know. We met about a year ago. Anyway, I thought I might come over and take care of the baby while you watch."

5. Flight

The cab had just come to a stop in front of the police station when Elaine handed the driver a twenty, picked up Ellen and her purse, shoved the door open and rushed up the sidewalk to the entrance. Inside the desk officer stood up.

"I'm Elaine Atkinson. I called ahead for Detectives Greg Hudziak and Sal Veterello."

"Yes, this way. They are expecting you."

As she hurried down the hallway she instinctively looked back over her shoulder, scanning for any menacing face. Another officer appeared, offering to hold the baby while they talked, but Elaine reacted by tightening her hold on Ellen. The tall detective met her at the door.

"Greg, you heard what happened?"

He nodded and closed the door behind them. "Why don't you sit over here."

"How did he get my number? How? That was a private line."

"Sit down and let's walk through this slowly. You are absolutely sure it was his voice?"

"Are you crazy? No mistake. No mistake. How could I ever forget?" Her own voice was thin, her pacing agitated.

Detective Veterello spoke. "It is an important question. Just remember that your memory of his face, mannerisms, actual words has been sketchy. You could not identify our primary suspect from the line-up. So why would his voice be so clear? And how can you be sure it was not a low-life prankster?"

Elaine finally sat down, swept her hand through her tousled hair, tried to slow her breathing and focus carefully. After a minute: "I have told you that my visual memory switches from flashing white to a dense blackness in the middle of it all. But that voice, malevolent, without soul. . . I had never heard any voice so brutal, sadistic. I will never forget it. The voice on the phone was the voice in that room where Todd was killed."

The detectives studied her carefully. "Okay. Then if you listen, again, to that voice you will never forget, does it jog any other memories?"

"Like what?"

"Anything. Close your eyes and hear the voice in that room. This time do you hear any accent? Any specific words you might have forgotten? And if his face is too blurred to remember, maybe his voice draws you to some other part of him, maybe a tattoo on his arm, a logo on his shirt, a scar. . ."

After a brief effort Elaine shook her head. "No. Stop. I don't want to hear that voice."

Detective Hudziak walked over to the water cooler, his long strides befitting his height. And as always his voice was the more patient. "Let's look at this Elaine. Why do you think he called after all this time? Oh, I know, the article in the paper caught his attention. But he could have called before that if he really wanted to threaten you."

"How should I know? You are the detectives, the guys who decipher the motives, the mentality on the street. You tell me."

"Well it is a mystery. There could be a little positive sign in all of this, that maybe he has not thought of you any more until the newspaper article. You know, 'out of sight out of mind.' A full year and he made no contact. It could be that even since that call he has already moved on in some manner."

"I find no reassurance in that theory. And go back to my central question: how did he get my private, unlisted number? After the call I sat there staring at the phone, and then noticed that my number was on it. Right there in bold print. And then came the terrifying thought: 'he has been here and copied it.' That is when I called you."

"You can rule out that theory, that he has been in your apartment."

"How? Why?"

"Elaine, if he had been so determined to find your apartment and break in, he would have waited there until you came back. You would not be standing here now."

His words were supposed by be reassuring, but they only served to amplify her deep sense of dread. She needed to change the subject. "So, how did he get my unlisted number? You tell me."

"You got any ideas Sal?"

The younger detective walked to the window, then turned. "Well, first, the obvious. Who are the people who have your number?"

Elaine quickly scanned her memory. "Very few. Family members. Two girl friends from school. That's all. Oh, and Dr. Keith and you two."

"That's all? Okay, and how could the killer make contact with anyone on that detailed list? Even if a family member talked about you, how could he get the number from them?"

Elaine stood and again began pacing, her impatience and irritation most evident. "So look. This is your job. How does anyone access an unlisted telephone number? Who can do that?" Then a sudden, abrupt thought. "Can the police do that?"

The detectives looked at one another and then Greg answered carefully. "Yes, we are authorized to access and scrutinize unlisted numbers. The department must open up many security systems to do its job."

"So if this guy knew some cop, he could maybe finagle the situation, maybe fix things or contrive some scheme, and get the number."

The tall one frowned. "Such requests are on record and we will investigate that. But it is most unlikely. I have told you that we have a primary suspect, and believe me, he would have nothing to offer a crooked cop, and could never intimidate him."

Elaine's growing apprehension was immediately noticeable. Her shallow breathing increased in tempo, the tension even effecting Ellen who began to rouse from her sleep. Her phone number was not as private as she thought.

And the next question was logical. "Who else beside the police department can access unlisted numbers?"

The detectives paused. "Well, the telephone company obviously. They have strict regulations about giving out such information . . . "

Elaine was on her feet. "You mean any number of people in the whole telephone company could get my number or find someone who could?"

She did not really hear their response. Maybe cops would be too tough to be intimidated by this guy, or would not be bought off. But all the people in the phone company? Who knows? Maybe one of his drinking buddies works for the phone company, or knows someone who does.

Her life began, again, spinning out of control. Exposed to the whole city, she was utterly vulnerable and unprotected from that killer who could track her down whenever he wanted. She was not even safe here, at police headquarters.

To their protests, Elaine rose abruptly and headed for the door. "I have got to get out of here. I have got to get completely out of this town."

* * *

Elaine was not known to be impulsive. But she did have a way of being decisive. Even when cornered she could quickly measure the alternatives and choose what seemed to be the most promising. Sometimes sheer logic determined the course of action; other times intuition seemed to lead.

So in her urgency to move she found herself driving west toward Wheaton. Far in the dim recesses of her mind she remembered someone, somewhere, referring to the town as a place that was very conservative and wary. It only took her two days there to find the little brick duplex. It was quiet, unnoticed, in a working class neighborhood, across the street from a school. Little trees stood as sentries on the street. A streetlight was just three houses to the south, and she made a night trip back just to be certain it was working. Safe enough she guessed. The doors were double locked but the downstairs windows bothered her. She would get some kind of metal grill to put on them. It would have to be on the inside; if it were on the outside it would advertise her fear to the whole world.

She made the move. Yet all was not resolved. Her sleep was fitful. Sounds common and unnoticed in her community seized her attention like tiny, piercing alarms. The old house itself creaked and sighed as it settled into its later years. This she partly welcomed as she wanted nothing more than to settle in herself, to merge with earth and stone and old smells. To blend with the passing parade so as to be indistinct, unobserved. To bond with Ellen and just stay in the shadows.

Still the paradox developed. The more determined she was to become truly settled into a new life the more restless she became. She remembered Dr. Keith's reference to her being hyper-vigilant, which, while understandable, kept the adrenalin pumping at all hours. So maybe it was a mistake, or at least counterproductive, for her to lead such a solitary existence. Being a recluse again was to increase her sense of always being the fugitive, frightened by what lurked around every corner. This time it would be necessary to meet some neighbors.

At first it was not so difficult. Most all of the women on the street or at the market were immediately interested in the baby, happy to remember and talk about when they were young mothers. Honest folk, civil. Only two of the women were nosy and probed for more details, especially about the absent father. The men were usually polite in a quiet but cautious manner, producing a subtle vein of mutual suspicion. There were a number of references to church life and Elaine noted that their very traditional belief systems helped them reduce complicated issues down to simple rules. This, however, added to her familiar sense of isolation, of not really having core values in common with those around her.

The dissonance appeared on many fronts. Mornings, for example, had always been Elaine's favorite time of day: the early blush of pink on the azure horizon, the calm interlude before children awaken, and most especially the sweet birdsong just before dawn, the chorus so perfectly countenanced by the blanket of quietness all around. But now something was different. The songbirds were not welcomed. Their message was edged with impending darkness. Gradually she began to recover another piece of a memory. Those birds were singing in the predawn when the killer stepped out of the darkness. They were not to be trusted. In fact, she wondered, did they keep singing even when the gunshots shattered that morning's silence?

Dissonance again. A notice in the suburban newspaper caught her eye, an announcement of a widow's group that met every month. That word "widow." Elaine realized that she had now been a widow almost as long as she had been married. So her interest in this group was immediate. She imagined talking with others, wondering about their losses, what she might say or do if she discovered another woman whose husband had been murdered. But upon arrival her high hopes were quickly deflated. The gathering was in a church hall where it looked as if almost thirty women were going to share their covered dishes for lunch. And then came the stunning realization which brought her to a complete stop: she was the youngest widow by at least thirty years. She turned and walked away.

The following weeks revolved like a hamster on a wheel, Elaine trying to move forward but seemingly getting nowhere. The sense of isolation was too familiar, the growing detachment too dangerous. But connections seemed simply unavailable. Discouragement was a constant shadow, increasing her awareness of fatigue and emptiness. Even her limbs seemed clumsy, a bit uncoordinated. She was finding it difficult to be attentive to Ellen's needs, impatient when she was fussy.

In therapy Elaine described her status, summing it up as "some instability." But Dr. Keith was immediate in his response. "No, Elaine, this is more than just feeling wobbly. You are depressed, on track into a major depression. Neither you nor Ellen can tolerate that. I am going to insist, yes insist that you begin taking an anti-depressant. You refused it before because of the pregnancy, but now we cannot compromise. We will initiate a tricyclic, Imipramine. I think you will find that it helps you with your sleep problem as well."

In the days that followed Elaine had a mixed reaction to the medication. To her surprise it was somewhat effective, slowing down the cinema of her life so that she could focus on it frame by frame. It brought relief. Yet it dulled her wits, and mornings were thick, sodden with the night. The dry mouth was a constant signal of her psychiatric status, her emotional disability. A mental patient.

She had to find a way to fight back, to counter this loss of her strong self. Once she told Dr. Keith "It seems like ages since I have had intelligent adult conversation." Dr. Keith held a steady course, reassuring her of emerging stability, encouraging her to pursue this insight. As a result she eventually checked into a local community college, telling the admissions clerk "I will take any class so long as it gets my mind on the rest of the world."

The very idea of returning to the classroom produced a sudden flood of new energy. This was the first positive excitement of recent memory and it soon evolved into a commitment. She would do it! But then how could she go to class if she always had Ellen with her? She had trusted no one until now to care for Ellen privately. It was perplexing. But when she tried to dismiss further education as impractical she started to feel immobilized, as if confined to a small cell of a lifeless prison. After several days she called Dr. Keith for an appointment. And again he was firm in his response. "Elaine, the time has come for you to move forward. You can no longer stand guard over your daughter day and night. You are ready to be reasonable and to recognize trustworthy persons. Let me make a call and I will get back to you how to proceed."

Five days later Dr. Keith called to arrange for Elaine to have an appointment at a pleasant office near a college campus in Wheaton. This was an agency with the enigmatic name "Familia." She was met by the director, Mrs. Marone, a pleasant woman likely in her mid-forties, neatly dressed, who invited her into her quiet office where she offered coffee and a choice of easy chairs. She explained that Familia was not just a child care service or an agency of certified nannies. Instead it sought to identify with a modern family which cannot provide constant parental care, support and supervision. Its origin was in Europe, primarily Italy, where the extended family had historically served to assist with the several children of any member. But times had changed, family clans were no longer intact, and agencies emerged which had to resemble the extended family in values and commitment. And so Familia had been established. It solicited skilled providers who would study the family they served, assimilate and reinforce those values with a high commitment to communication and building trust as an extended family member. Only then would the child care begin. This was true whether it was only for occasional extended weekends, or daily care, or residing in the family home as a primary parent figure.

Elaine was reassured by the Director's intelligence and sincerity. Mrs. Marone would personally want to meet Ellen, fully understand the needs for mother and daughter, gain clarity on Elaine's values and goals, and then search through her roster of providers to see if a match could be found. If so Elaine would then personally interview the provider until trust was established and then observe the interaction as she met Ellen. Only then would the contract be drawn and the specific expectations defined. As she left the meeting Elaine was surprised that she was able to even consider the idea of leaving Ellen with another woman.

And so the process began. There was an initial consultation fee which Elaine initially felt was inflated, but once Mrs. Marone met Ellen it was apparent that a comprehensive effort would be made to see if the right provider could be found and would meet Elaine's expectations. Several weeks passed and Elaine began to wonder if her needs were too specific or demanding for any provider. But then the call came. And Elaine was to meet Carolyn, a woman in her fifties, a single mother of two children who had now both married and moved away, one to Seattle and the other to Charleston. As a mother she had closely participated in their development, reading to them, stimulating them with challenges, supporting their separate interests. She had heard of Familia and when her own nest emptied she offered her credentials as an established parent. She could find other employment but she considered her gift for appreciating child development as being that which she would pursue.

And Elaine found Carolyn to be an excellent and most acceptable fit. She was without pretense, projecting a combination of genuine kindness, strength, and the desire to play a vital role in this family of two. She would be able to come to Elaine's home when necessary, or have Ellen come to her home. It would be expensive but there could be no investment more important. And, as Elaine would reflect years later, it was this one decision which was to fully open the door for a new life and profession.

* * *

August 1983

"So the detectives are trying to persuade you to submit to hypnosis to stimulate your memory, and you are pretty resistant."

Elaine frowned. "Well, of course. You and I have completely searched that memory bank. Don't you think so? Would you recommend I go through all of that again? What would some other psychiatrist say?"

A long pause. "Well, I am of two opinions. On the one hand, I have experienced you as determined and willing to recover any memory, even when it was a dreadful thing to relive, and you now have every right to move forward into a new chapter of your life and work to put this nightmare behind you. On the other hand, the police now have a primary suspect. Their street informer heard the guy give details that only the killer could have. But they still don't have the hard evidence to make an arrest. The informer would never testify and even if he did he would not be a credible witness to the court. So they think if you could recover anything new which might ensure his identity, then he would be out of your life forever."

Dr. Keith focused on his own tension. He felt protective of her, noting how she was always looking over her shoulder. No wonder her sleep was fitful. There was no stillness in her life.

A long pause. Finally: "If you were to agree I would want a colleague of mine to do the hypnosis. I don't know this police psychologist."

"But you have said on a number of occasions that it might be in my interest to simply bury certain specific memories, maybe details so horrible that I just put them away."

"That's true. All of us repress some things in order to survive."

"Hmm. 'Survive.' That's it, isn't it. Survive. That's what it comes down to. I am a survivalist. I don't live to fulfill my potential, to have life more abundantly. I live to survive. To hide from the hunter in this darkened wasteland."

* * *

It took only three months for her to realize this move was a mistake. Her hyper-vigilance had remained constant and she believed that iron grids on the downstairs windows could easily be kicked in. And any safety she had hoped for in this neighborhood was offset by the cultural dissonance. She had little in common with these people. It was necessary to move again, this time across town to the upstairs of a larger house, the downstairs occupied by some older couple who stayed to themselves.

Being upstairs brought back memories of the first days with Ellen at Dave and Barbara's. That safety and privacy brought momentary respite and she turned her attention to decorating a small nursery. At a small shop she bought a mobile of stars to hang over Ellen's playpen to the tune of "It's a Small World". Ellen was exploring all of her toys but seemed to prefer kitchen utensils most of all. She seemed to be in constant motion, eagerly clapping the tray of her new high chair as she sought to feed herself, delighting in putting a Halloween witches hat on her head. And fussy when she was getting no attention.

And so it was time to call Carolyn for the initial scheduling of visits. As they worked together Ellen found Carolyn to be a calming and patient figure, a contrast to the stress and impatience she experienced in her mother. And this did not escape Elaine's notice. It was time to move forward, now, with her re-entry into college.

Her classes at the little community college, originally sought as a kind of diversion, now turned out to be stimulating. In her brief college experience she had enjoyed her studies in psychology, and now her own psychotherapy transformed abstract theory into vital, living questions. Clearly if she were to rebuild her life she needed to return to Illinois-Chicago and complete her undergraduate work. It would be demanding, commuting three days each week in all kinds of weather. Carolyn would now play a vital role in allowing Elaine to devote full time to her studies.

She was determined. She enrolled and accepted the challenge. Todd had believed in her and she would prove him right. But she underestimated the stress which soon seemed to be pushing into her from every direction. The travel. Ellen's demands. The hypnotism experiment which was two hours of torment, yielding nothing new. The detectives, calling her in for more mug shots, and their disturbing, alarming new manner of referring to the killer by name. They knew who he was and where he lived. They simply did not have evidence to convict him.

And then there was the stress of her therapy. In Dr. Keith's office she noted a phrase on a collage attributed to someone named Perls. It read: "To suffer one's death in order to be reborn is not easy."

* * *

December, 1983

"Elaine, when I point out your resistance to something, you get defensive as if I am accusing you of some weakness. Again I say, all therapy moves forward at the point of resistance, opening up and hopefully appropriating some important new area of what has previously been uncovered."

"Like what?"

"Oh, your mother for instance. You never mention her without some side inflection, some gesture. Rolling your eyes. Or your father who might be the greater mystery. You never mention him at all."

"My father? That's pretty simple. He committed suicide."

"What?"

"Yeah, killed himself."

"Your father? Oh, I had no idea."

"I think that is when my younger sister Sarah and actually the whole family learned to talk casually about suicide, as if it were almost routine."

A long pause. "How old were you?"

"Let's see, I was fifteen."

"Can you talk about what happened?"

"He shot himself."

"I mean did you see this coming? What was it like for you?"

She paused to bring the sequences together. "Well, he left us when I was around eleven. He'd just had enough. Things at home had become God-awful, all the screaming between my parents, then the long silent treatments. I remember I was having a migraine every day that year. He had a girlfriend, Betty, who was mother's arch-nemesis from high school days. Mother would sometimes call her and threaten to kill her. I remember as if it were yesterday: 'Leave him alone or I will come over and kill you.' And I remember one time at the art museum where my brother's paintings were being shown. Dad and Betty came. And in public mother screamed 'What is he doing here with his fucking whore.' I just wanted to be invisible."

"Eleven years old, caught in the middle of a grinding . . . "

"Oh I didn't blame him for leaving mother. He would periodically come over and visit us kids. But gradually it felt like he had abandoned us for Betty, and that made me furious. For Betty! By the way, she became paranoid schizophrenic in the days ahead."

"And then, three years later, out of the blue you have to look that devil in the eye called suicide."

"Well, it was not entirely out of the blue. Mother attempted suicide several times before that. One day she took a bottle of pills, spilled a lot of them on the floor, made me pick them up, and kicked me when I was too slow. I picked them up but thought 'okay, if you want to do this, then go ahead.' And she did. Then the ambulance came and I watched them take her away. But soon they sent her back home. They always sent her back home. Just pump her stomach and send her back home."

* * *

November, 1983

She finally looked up, intensely studying the face of Dr. Keith.

"What is it Elaine? I don't want to intrude into your silence, but you have been struggling with something for several minutes. What is going on?"

"The last session it was easy to talk about my father compared to talking about my mother. There are things maybe better left alone, things I have never talked about to anyone, except some of it with Todd or Brian. And how can I just suddenly trust you?"

"Suddenly? We have worked together many hours now."

"But not about my earliest years."

"Sounds critically important. You are fearful of revisiting that, yet I feel that you want to."

"No. I certainly don't want to. But maybe I need to. To go through the eye of the storm as they say."

He nods.

She speaks after a deep breath. "Okay. My childhood was just gritting my teeth, sometimes doing my best to be invisible, and sometimes tolerating random punishment for things I didn't do. And then even when she discovered the truth mother would not apologize. I had nightmares as a kid. She was impulsive, not logical, so those dreams seemed possible. She had a big butcher knife with a pink handle. I would dream that she had decapitated Brian and was coming after me."

He observes that she is holding herself with her arms tightly across her chest, and rocking. "That had to be terrifying for a little girl."

"I wanted to start school and get away from home. But I really wasn't into school. There was this nun at school who said that un-baptized babies would not be admitted to heaven but would be exiled to some dead place called limbo. I said that I could not believe that God would punish a baby for something the parents never did. She shrugged and said, simply: 'That's just the way it is.' From that point on I would just memorize doctrine and not believe it. If things made no sense I would just say 'That's just the way it is.' That's what I would try to do with the bad stuff."

A field of intense energy filling the room. "The bad stuff?"

Slowly. "It started happening after mother's father died. She hated him; he had molested her as a little girl and was abusive over the years. And so on the weekends, when Dad had a part-time job, she would call Sarah and me into the bedroom and shut the door. I was around seven, Sarah was three or four. She ordered us to be naked on the bed from the waist down. She would sit on the floor beside us. Because of what her father did to her as a little girl, she wanted to make sure we were not 'dirty down there.' She said, 'I am cleaning you' and would examine us with a corsage pin, poking the sharp end into all the nooks and crannies. When she would stick us and it hurt, we were not allowed to cry. Her warning was severe: 'Quit crying or I will lock you in the closet again.' And so it was on those dreaded Saturdays."

"Dear God." There is a long, still pause. "You kept this all to yourself?"

"Dad was gone. The boys were out doing lawn work. The older girls were running the sweepers. Brian would sometimes sit on the other side of the door. He once heard one of us say 'not the needles please!' and remembered being glad he was not a girl."

"How long did this go on?"

"Most of two years. Until Dad lost his Saturday job."

"Elaine, how did you manage to survive this?"

"There's that word again. Survive." She is thoughtful, carefully composing her words. "Remember when I told you about those self-hypnosis things, like in the hospital when I disappeared, off on a trip into the waters, or at the funeral when I left that place and let myself be lifted away by the blue arms of the stained glass lights in the church. The wormhole. Well, I guess these times were when I learned that. When mother would start in, I would look over to my right across the bedroom. There was an Avon bottle there, some kind of perfume. It was rose colored. And it was placed in just such a way that the light from outside somehow focused like a laser on it, and it refracted that light into long fingers on the walls, and fans splayed on the ceiling. And I learned to leave behind the blood of my pink skin and be joined with the soft rose hues which were gently beckoning to me. And then my soul would be invisible to mother and the world."

* * *

The curtain of December opened into a colder darkness, a pervasive emptiness, a dangerous will. Elaine felt overwhelmed by it all, helplessly observing her depression deepening, her anxiety increasing to inner screams. She sat on the edge of her bed looking out with a grey stare, the moon on her ghostly face. Outside the snows had carved the landscape into a giant white chalk fortress, occasional people moving by lifeless, their faces like marble, their steps like small sharp bones snapping.

The pathways of her life, so deliberately charted, now seemed hopelessly entangled. She squeezed her eyes shut, took a deep breath, and tried to find some direction, and beginning with a new and even safer place to live. In the midst of her busy studies and with Carolyn's help she searched other subdivisions of Wheaton until she finally found what looked secure and comfortable. Over a long weekend she found the time to pack and mustered the energy to move once again. Now she was on the third floor of a five-story apartment building which had been converted to condominiums. It was supposed to provide, finally, a fortress in her miniature world. But as the weeks passed the stress did not abate. Her hyper-vigilance had reached new heights, especially when she had to walk across campus for night classes. Now her back pack consisted of a calculus text, a chemistry text, mace and a butcher knife. And endless snacks as she continued to eat and eat and gain more and more weight.

The therapy, which was supposed to bring relief, was now a mixed blessing. She did find hope as Dr. Keith guided her through the analytic wilderness with the promise that the light of day would open into what had been hidden in the darkness. But it seemed to increase her sense of instability. The more she remembered and described her childhood and family interaction, and the more her medication brought her mind to a clear and exact focus, it could not be denied: the family home had been a very crazy, perilous place. She saw the look on Dr. Keith's face when she recounted Brian's story, when he was five years old, of being told by mother to pull down his pants and expose his genitals to her amused women friends. Or mother accusing Elaine of "most assuredly" having sex behind the bushes with the boys of the neighborhood. And later mother again, telling her and her sisters that the onset of menses likely meant cancer. Dr. Keith had explained that mother was most likely a Borderline Personality Disorder. But Elaine was left to dread the possibility that such a diseased mind could be passed on to her.

She looked over at the sleeping Ellen. Here was a major concern. She had been a quick child, bright and verbal, seemingly presenting two or three new words a day. Her curiosity, delight in anything new, and the pleasure she took in games with mother had become her character. But now things seemed to be changing. She cried frequently, was fussy and no longer found inspiration in things which were once exciting. Carolyn seemed to have a way of lifting her spirits. It had been her idea which resulted in the first birthday cake. Ellen had been transfixed by the one little candle flame for a blessed moment. And she had watched and wondered as her mother and Carolyn sang to her, and laughed, and huddled in a rare celebration. But then when just the two of them were left alone Ellen seemed unhappy. Elaine began to conclude that the demon of depression which was consuming her was now infecting her daughter. She began to revisit a thought she had previously entertained: that if mother could not pull herself out of the downward spiral, maybe she should begin to arrange for Ellen's adoption. Ellen would be too young to be traumatized by her mother's suicide.

Outside, the winds of the world were being sucked into town. The poplar trees shivered across from the window.

Roofs creaked. Nearby ruins emerged from shadows. She turned to take extra medication, wishing to ride a gentle boat into the waters of easy sleep. But she knew it would not be so. Her sleep would be familiar episodes of embracing the growing madness.

* * *

The last time Elaine had seen the detectives was at that ill-fated hypnosis session. They had brought pictures, more vivid this time, from the murder scene, hoping to activate her memory with new evidence for them to use against the killer. They had apologized for the pain that it caused her. Now they wanted to see her again, hoping to reassure her. Maybe a warm spot in a cold, grey February.

"We wanted you to see his rap sheet. This is his name, face, history. Twenty-seven years old. Lives with his family. You were not able to pick him out of a line-up on two occasions. You were being honest; you said he looked similar but you could not be certain. So here he is. Mile long record for burglary, assault and armed robbery. Your house was in his territory and it is most certain that he spotted Todd at the doughnut shop. We guess he was startled when Brian suddenly came into the room and pulled the trigger impulsively. Then he had to take care of witnesses."

Elaine had often privately castigated herself for not being able to pick him out of the line-up. Because she was dazed? Or inept? Or simply afraid? That inner recitation now returned with such heaviness that she slumped, feeling the intrusion of the hopelessness she had so long fought.

The detectives studied her, then one another, then looked away. After an interlude Detective Hudziak spoke. "Elaine, we want you to understand something. This is a bad guy. We know he did this but we can't grab him. He knows that and lets us know that he got away with it." The detective then paused, took a deep breath, looked for an instant at his partner, they continued. "Anyway, if something happened to the two of us, we were transferred or something and the case went cold, well that is not acceptable. We hope someone takes him out. He needs to be taken care of."

Elaine was stunned. Detective Hudziak was immobile, his eyes locked on her. The light of the room in that hour framed him for her to scrutinize. The clear radar of her mind focused on his hidden message. Finally she spoke. "Greg, say exactly what you mean?"

"You understand that I would deny saying this. But the truth is if someone else took this guy out, we would look the other way. At least not investigate the killing with any tenacity. Someone would be doing the world a big favor."

Elaine held his eyes in the connection with hers. The room was thick with tension. The detectives were frozen warriors, their faces ascetic. Elaine felt herself to be a stone of silence in their midst. Her mind was precisely focusing. She would need to do it herself. And this must be her most private counsel. Finally she rose from her chair. "I need to be alone and consider this."

* * *

It was after lunch that she went to the bank, then hailed a cab. When she told the cab driver to take her to a gun store, he hesitated to drive away, looking at her in his rear-view mirror. Something about the way she said the word "gun." She read his mind and smiled. "Nothing to worry about. I need to talk to the proprietor about a birthday present for my husband. He is a hunter."

They pulled up to a small box building, white concrete block, across the street from an small older shopping mall. The large windows featured sales and bargains notices. She paid her fare and went inside. It was darker than usual, the windows all being tinted to provide a semi-secrecy to transactions within. The clerk was occupied with a customer, giving her time to browse. She quickly found the display of handguns in the glass case. Some with long barrels, some with silver handles, some with revolving chambers. And then those two. They looked familiar. She shuddered slightly. And what was that smell? A moth smell blended with a hint of gun oil, or was it gunpowder? She translated the smell to the clothes he wore and the acrid spray from the gunfire. A wave of nausea drifted over her and she stepped away, into a corner. Now horrible thoughts emerged. How could she think of pulling the trigger of that gun? To do what he did. What was wrong with her? Was she now becoming a psychopath like him?

The clerk took notice and started to speak to her as she turned away, but it was too late. She pushed open the stiff door, heavy with locks and bars, filled her lungs with the fresh air, then walked immediately across the street, wanting to quickly lose herself in the anonymity of a shopper's mall.

* * *

February, 1984

Elaine was pacing back and forth, from office chair to the window and back again. Her movement was grizzled, her hand repeatedly combing through her hair, the other fist clenched.

"Don't you understand? I really do want to kill him, and that makes me no different than he is. I must forfeit my outrage because I spit the same venom."

"Stop Elaine! What are you doing? What kind of a delusion is this, that you are like him? You are as different from him as a bird is from a fish. And what narcissism is it that demands that you should never have a thought of wishing someone were dead? That is common, basically human stuff for all of us."

She did stop, turned and observed her doctor. Then she moved closer, scrutinizing him. Her mind was clear like a quiet stream, and he seemed ready to swallow the truth like water. Quite deliberately she walked to her chair, pushed it closer to him, sat down, folded her hands, and began "Are you ready for this? Okay. Tell me if you want me to stop, to muffle the truth. Okay?"

Dr. Keith nodded, holding her face with his eyes.

"You say my thoughts are basic, common human stuff, like 'I would like to wring his neck'? Oh no. That is mild. Let me tell you. I imagine, again and again, of not just killing him but of first torturing him. Is the word torture even strong enough?" Her words are calm, carefully chosen and fitted. "I imagine having him immobile so I can shave his skin off, one millimeter at a time. He would scream until I stuffed a sock in his mouth. He has a lot of skin and there is a lot of blood on it. And then after a while I would cut off his cock. I would tie off the artery so he doesn't bleed out on me. While he watched I would boil it, take out the cock and make him eat it."

Elaine halted, studying her doctor. He was skilled at being imperturbable. Very well, she would continue. "He would beg me to stop. I would remind him he never thought of stopping with Todd or Brian. After a while his pain is unbearable and he is now asking me to finish him off. I do, but slowly. I have an axe and I chop off all extremities, one arm, then the other, then one leg, then the other. He dies. But it is not enough. Now I begin to dice him. Dice him. After most of an hour of hard work he begins to look like road kill. But an unrecognizable species."

There is a long silence. Her face is like marble, her breathing shallow. His face is supple but strong, his breathing slow and normal. She waits for a reaction she can reject. He waits for her to say or do whatever is now needed.

After several minutes she must connect in some recognizable form.

"So, there. Now you really know me. Hardly common human stuff would you say." No response. Then "Well doctor, what do you say?"

His words bear both the firmness and affection of sincerity. "I am deeply touched that you can share with me this depth of your passion. Thank you. I have always wondered how you have endured your suffering. You have such strength at your core."

The room seemed to be in motion, shifting to confusing winds and clouds. Elaine, withdrew, now hugging herself, alone in her chair. Did he fail to hear her?

"How can you be so calm? Are you used to this kind of psychotic muck?"

"It is not psychotic at all, Elaine. It is the expression of the wound that exists deep in your soul. It might become psychotic if you just left it there to fester. Now you have opened it to the possibility of healing. You have the gift of such courage."

* * *

It seemed that her world really was beginning to stabilize. The confusion would appear in mood shifts. One minute she would comprehend that her ability to claim the full depth of her rage was honest, that the energy used for former repression was now released for her use with real choices. She was free, in fact, to do anything she wanted provided she would endure the consequences. And the consequences of actually torturing and killing that man would ultimately be dire, legally and spiritually. But then would come another minute when she believed she was kidding herself, that anyone who could have such rage was primitive, crazy, in fact a large and dangerous animal. Her therapy supported the former hypothesis; her occasional nightmares the latter.

If there were good news it was the termination of what had been an endless winter. She had actually forgotten that the greening season was hidden in the grey. But now springtime beckoned, a soft and melting transition, and the morning crept up on her, unnoticed, when she heard the first birdsong at four a.m. That song always brought both a smile and a frown.

The fresh days of the world outside were countered by the grinding days inside. School was intense, classrooms were demanding, libraries were tedious. And Ellen continued to be upset, irritated by first one thing, then discouraged by another. Elaine continued to sense that the child was feeding off the mother's depression.

Access to the name of the killer was frequently on Elaine's mind. They said he was married. What kind of wife would be with him? What kind of parents endured him? One question would prompt another until she would finally just resolve to push it all to the back shelf and stay with the tasks at hand.

Or so it was until one day in the lobby of her building was a stack of new phone books, one for each resident. As she carried hers into her unit she had a sudden thought: "I wonder if his name is in the phone book?" She found it strange that she had not considered this before. Dr. Keith would say she was repressing it, not really wanting such information. But now she wondered. And she looked. And everything stopped. Her life compressed into an electric moment. There was his name! And the address? She was aghast. It was less than one mile away from where they had lived on Cullerton. And only a few miles now. He was always out there, a mile or two away.

Elaine called Dr. Keith for an immediate appointment. He could see her the next day. When she explained her situation he was puzzled. What difference, really, did it make if he lived a mile away or thirty miles away? The people from his neighborhood did not come over to Wheaton for their shopping and he certainly did not attend any of her social venues. And, further, she had already made the decision not to kill him or have him killed. The only thing new was that she knew precisely where she could drive by if she so desired. And did she want to do that? In truth her curiosity did not desire to see his house or his family. It left her edgy knowing that, on some impulse, she might go look. But she also trusted her emerging sense of self-direction, and she had never been impulsive. She took a deeper breath of confidence.

She had turned her full attention to approaching finals at school, undistracted, until the phone rang one morning. It was Detective Hudziak again, this time having no apparent agenda to reassure or support Elaine but rather on official business. Could she drop by today for another mug shot? She agreed, fitting the business into her early afternoon schedule.

Elaine greeted several persons by name as she entered the precinct station. As she walked down the hall she wondered for a moment just how many times she had been there. And then there was the most recent time which had confounded her. And they were just trying to help. And now they wanted her to help them.

The photo she was to study was, on this occasion, not the usual mug shot. It was, instead, the picture of a guy who was dead, on a slab at the morgue. And the question: "Does this look like the killer?"

She looked at both detectives quizzically. If this were her killer they would be announcing the good news. So why this? She suspended her question and looked again, purely objective. After a minute she said "No. There are some similar features, but this is not him."

The detective clarified: "So you have never seen this man before?"

She frowned. "No. Why would you ask that?"

"Well, this is his brother. There was always the forensic possibility that it could have been his brother."

"This is, was, his brother? His brother? What happened? How did he die?"

"The police came to his place with an arrest warrant for murder. He saw them, fired a shot and tried to escape. They returned fire and killed him."

She was speechless. Both brothers were killers. Both.

"We also wanted you to know so you were not surprised. His parents came with some others to claim police brutality. It will be on the news tonight."

She could not study the remainder of the day, and her attention to Ellen was sporadic. Then, finally, came the local news. It was the third report before any commercial. There they were, the actual parents, being interviewed by a reporter. Their words were frequently bleeped out, apparent profanity. But their rage was lethal.

The private winds of detachment began to quicken in the hours that followed. She was in a daze. Sounds seemed muffled, her own speech to Ellen slurred. This was not irony but mockery. These foul parents defending this man who shot at the police. These humans who had birthed and raised two males who preyed on some and killed others. This low life.

She paced the floor all evening, sometimes oblivious to Ellen. This was really happening and she no longer knew how to cope with it. A pervasive numbness presented itself, slowly expanding, spreading its veins to her extremities, to her gut and to her face. From somewhere came the old invitation to disappear, to dissociate and leave this place where life is cheap. But she could not leave Ellen who, in this moment, was being fed.

The old psychic detachment was familiar. But she was in touch with reality, and she was putting Ellen to sleep, however clumsily. She watched her daughter drift off, reflecting that perhaps Ellen was the last person she would ever love. She felt unable to love other humans. People like those parents, popping out babies that will grow into killer boys like theirs. How many families like that are there, spread across this earth? Who would they murder tonight? How to have even a touch of good will for society? It was a ruthless, cutthroat world from which she felt an expanding estrangement. She watched the trees in the streetlights and found herself no longer caring for the earth itself. A perimeter of sadness bordered all its fields. The highest trees bore mortal wounds. Melancholic winds were becoming permanent and final.

Elaine tried and tried to sleep but without even a chance of success. She was not only depressed, but now defeated. Her interest in life was diminishing by the hour, and the thought of attempting to focus on and coordinate a new morning seemed now beyond all hope. Old familiar thoughts of suicide reappeared, this time not as some savage reprisal but as blessed relief. She was tired beyond measure, indifferent, her only connection being to her daughter.

And how about her daughter? She was the product of unleashed passions, having no say about entry into this world. And now she was supposed to grow up in it, dare to trust and have hopes, only to see them suddenly smashed by some savage animal. We put to sleep small animals that for whatever reason cannot survive. So that would be the last act of love Elaine would ever express.

But how to do that? She could smother her. But Elaine would be awake long enough to know, somehow, that her own mother had turned to attack her. She could drown her in the bathtub. That's it. Ellen would be upside down in a strange environment, disoriented, quickly aspirating the water, quickly unconscious.

Elaine sat up in bed. Somewhere tears were still produced in her. The pain of her being overwhelmed returned and the core of her being welcomed it. She could not dissociate this time. For the sake of this innocent child she had to endure being totally forsaken on this planet. She must stay sane, somehow, until the morning.

Elaine later reported that she does not remember how she kept going. She came to herself precisely at 7 A.M. when she called Dr. Keith.

"I need to see you. Right now! All night I have been feeling suicidal and homicidal."

"Why didn't you go immediately to the E.R.?"

"It never occurred to me. Mother was often suicidal and went to the E.R. Nothing happened. They would just send her home again. If they sent me back that would be the end for both of us."

"Okay, then you agree that you need to go to the hospital."

"Oh yes. Oh yes."

"You have two immediate tasks. One, pack a bag with some clothes and toiletries. That won't take but a minute or two. Then leave a message for Carolyn to come to the hospital for Ellen. Can you do that one quickly?"

From utter exhaustion she was heard to say "I promise."

6. Transformation

Eight weeks in the hospital at Rush had been a long, long time. Night after night she reviewed all the events which had brought about her improvement: the sessions with Dr. Keith; the group therapy; the interventions and confrontations; the medications; the kindness and care from the staff who related so quickly to Carolyn and worked out plans for her to see Ellen daily; the cooperation of the university so she could complete her classes later; the support of two friends from school; and early permission to leave the hospital for blocks of time, returning in the evening. Eight weeks that would be forever etched in her life memory.

She remembered how things had not started off well. The intake nurse apparently failed to read summary orders from Dr. Keith and in her oblivion asked "Why are you here? Are you depressed? Are you having trouble with your husband?" Elaine was outraged at the stupidity, the insensitivity. Then a medical student was assigned to give her a physical. His hands were trembling and when she instructed him to forego any pelvic examination he was confused, telling the intake nurse he could not proceed. These two events apparently were so unsettling to the nurse that she assigned Elaine to a restricted unit, this in spite of her being a voluntary admission seeking solitude. And on that restricted unit she found herself with a bizarre roommate who huddled in the corner, murmuring in continual dialogue with mysterious figures, and who became terrified if the lights were ever turned out.

It took most of the first two days to disentangle, two days before she could seek refuge, alone in a private room. When she shut the door, a wave of blessed relief swept over her. Unlike her house where she had been increasingly hyper-vigilant, every night checking under the bed and leaving a small light on in the closet, here the fear abated. Here there was security. And safety now for Ellen, being separated at night from a mother with suicidal tendencies.

Most of the first week was a blurred memory, a twilight retreat. The nurses said that she was not sedated, but she slept for long periods. Perhaps it was the relief, perhaps the medication for both depression and anxiety. They would wake her when Ellen was brought over – sweet Ellen whose cheerfulness with Carolyn changed to a kind of somberness when she was brought to her mother's room.

Gradually Elaine began to reclaim her focus and concluded that it was the right decision to come here. In spite of the initial foul-ups, the professional staff was competent and generally sincere. Some of the doctors seemed a bit remote and distant, details that she enjoyed reporting back to Dr. Keith in their daily therapy. But two or three of the nurses were particularly helpful: respectful, kind, gentle, understanding. And so non-judgmental. When she learned that her mother was wanting to visit, Elaine turned immediately to one nurse, adamant that mother not be allowed in the unit. The nurse's response was firm: "You bet." When mother would send cards and flowers, Elaine interpreted this. "She knows I am going to talk about her and she wants to look good." The nurse smiled and nodded.

Months later, as she analyzed the hours and days and weeks of her treatment, Elaine was clear about something else: this was a place of potential healing relationships, and some of the most powerful were discovered with the house staff, the non-professionals who cleaned the rooms, prepared and brought the food, changed linens, ran errands and made repairs. There was a transparent honesty to them, like country music, a lack of pretense. They had no access to psychiatric categories or complex therapeutic strategies. But they brought a perspective born of simple and sometimes very old wisdom.

She thought of Imogene, a woman in her fifties, her strong appearance and step enhanced by a broad frame, her skin black satin, who came daily for general housekeeping. Her full black hair was always brushed to a sheen. But it was the way she would touch persons with her clear eyes and soothe them with her calming smile that revealed the powerful presence of someone deeply active in a soulful world. Even when she would enter the room with a genuine "Good Morning!" or go immediately to adjust the blinds to allow more light, there was a quiet purpose and command. As she moved about, she hummed little songs to herself, unobtrusive, orchestrated with her own rhythms. And she was highly observant. Elaine smiled remembering the time when the television was airing someone's point of view, and from the bathroom she heard Imogene's philosophical chuckle about that man taking himself too seriously.

Imogene could sense things, then know the intricate timing of when to address them. One afternoon, hours after she had cleaned the room, she returned, expecting Elaine to be sitting in the dark, not surprised to find her quietly weeping. She had seen it coming that morning. "What's wrong honey?"

Elaine sobbed softly, re-composed herself, and then said it. "It's no use. I try to bounce back but there is not much left. I don't want to live anymore. I think of ways of ending it."

Imogene nodded, took her hand, rocked slightly in her chair, the soft hum returning like some old hymn. "Oh no, honey. Can't do that. Even though you are worn out. It's when we have no strength left at all that the Lord restores us. That's his promise."

Elaine looked up, a bit stunned. Ordinarily she would have had no patience with religious slogans, with simple-minded solutions to convoluted issues. But then, again, this was not a simple faith. It came from some unfathomable depth in her life. She studied her intently, then answered honestly. "Imogene, you do understand that I don't want to live anymore."

The small humming and rocking continued while she took Elaine's hand into both of hers. "Yes child. It is cold there isn't it. Empty and cold. I know that place. And our Lord knew it in Gethsemane. He felt truly forsaken. Felt life was pointless. That he had been a fool. Completely defeated.

But he didn't quit. No, he didn't quit. And we can't quit either. Can't do that. You take his hand and you will surely see the Resurrection."

She then rose quietly, turned and placed a small embroidered bookmark on the pillow and left silently. Elaine looked at the words. "I am with you always, even unto the end of the world."

That memory still was touching, all these months later. Imogene. She never referred to Elaine's desire to die again as if their moment had been in a confessional. But her mystic smile, inner songs, and confident steps were constant. And the memory precipitated a thought: "Hmm. They don't have anything in this class on psychotherapy about spiritual resourcing. Psycho-therapy: doesn't that mean 'soul work'?"

Back to healing relationships: Mr. Boggs. Hard to guess his age, somewhere between 45 and 65. A wiry man, a bit taller than others, bespectacled. From the maintenance department he always wore a jump suit. He had a shop down next to the furnace room but it was hard to imagine how much work he accomplished there because a call for him was usually forthcoming two or three times a day. He would always arrive at the scene of the problem with energy born of great interest. Like a detective, he searched for clues for the cause of the crime. Or, like a surgeon, he carefully, methodically surveyed the malfunctioning component, plotting his course of remedial action. Or, like an inventor, he analyzed the need to build, on the spot, a part that had not before been created.

These features of Mr. Boggs were of interest to Elaine and to others because his entire approach to his work reflected his life philosophy: things break all the time and simply need to be repaired. Things and people. Nothing lasts and we need not take it personally when the malfunction occurs, when the system overloads. As for people, everybody has something that does not work, often several things, and the challenge is to analyze the breakdown and get things going again.

6. TRANSFORMATION

Dear Mr. Boggs. Always friendly, always curious about the course of the chess or Scrabble game in the community room, always hospitable and eager to accommodate special needs. But never any pity. He was a subtle inspiration in his work, a reminder that confidence shall prevail. Residents would watch him up on the ladder in the dining hall, diagnosing the recurrent problem with the central lighting, patiently persisting until it was fixed. All was well again as he believed it would be. Or when he would disassemble the window crank in a patient's room, examining and then with his file restoring the worn gears; and now the window could be opened. A wooden spindle on the staircase was somehow split; replacing it was easy but, because it was unpainted, he brought up a paint color spectrum until he found the precise match. Now it fit in perfectly.

Someone once asked Mr. Boggs if he had ever been stumped, or could he resolve every problem. The question brought him to a pause as he had not really considered ever being defeated. Then they reminded him that this was a hospital where all kinds of people came with all kinds of dysfunction; had he ever faced a big challenge? He thought for a while, then simply revealed that his wife suffered from diabetes and required daily insulin, that he had two stents in his heart from by-pass surgery five years ago, and that a boy in his neighborhood suffered a diving accident which left him paraplegic. But, no. Not defeated. Again, everybody has got something. The need is to bounce back and find a way to make things work.

Imogene. Mr. Boggs. The two other nurses. Healing relationships. And then there was Inez. Most of all the mysterious Inez. Her influence would extend far, far into Elaine's future. She worked as an art therapist in the activities program. Unlike the other professionals she had no academic degrees nor licenses, but unlike the house staff she had full access to the diagnoses and treatment plans of all patients who were released to activities. No clinical staff meeting would think of starting without her, and although she never offered her input unless requested, her insight was usually unique, and sometimes profound.

Inez often went unnoticed by patients, at least in their first days. It was her quiet way of calling no attention to herself. She moved about gently, drifting on the periphery of the room. She was the unit small shadow, at just over five feet in height, a diminutive and nameless secret. Her nationality was unclear: was she partly Asian, Hispanic, or even Native American? Her age was anyone's guess; her brown and coarse hair with grey strands rested unattended on her shoulders. Her face was even more indistinct, vague in general expression, unmarred by any lines of stress. Her grey eyes were inscrutable because they were frequently cast down, avoiding casual connection with the eyes of others. Yet when she would engage in a challenge to a patient to express the true idea or feeling inside, those eyes were pure radar, probing inner worlds.

Elaine came to the activities program late in her second week. When she inquired as to where she should start and for what purpose, Inez pointed to the art supplies and, with the gesture of a baker displaying her many cakes, invited her to make any choice. The first day she worked with modeling clay, forming farm animals which Ellen might enjoy when they visited. But as she worked she paid close attention to Ruth, the patient next to her, who was working with paints. And so the next day as Elaine started to continue with the clay, Inez's hand appeared over her shoulder with an array of paints and a canvas on an easel. Inez then moved away, saying not a word. Elaine thought for a moment about the power of intuition, then put away the clay and picked up the brush.

Her first attempts were for definitive figures: a building with trees, a storefront, a pastoral scene featuring a pond in a vernal wreath, crowned with pink clouds. But her dissatisfaction with the effort surged with a sudden exasperation so intense that she snapped her pencil. She stepped back to survey her pathetic paint production and with the wave of frustration and feelings of complete inadequacy she dipped her brush in heavy, thick black and slashed a large bar diagonally across paper. Inez appeared immediately, looked at the expression, and shook her head in strong approval. And then moved away. But Elaine got the cue. Go abstract, express emotion, energy, movement. Release. Let it go.

But the rush of excitement, the invitation to be open, was met instantly by a wave of fear. The voice – whose voice did it sound like? – was literal and distinct, reminding her that she must never lose control. She had survived by austere control. Then came the counterpoint, not so much a voice as a central truth: a promise that she could build a new and better life if she could claim her freedom. This was answered by a stern internal warning. The conflict left her confused and doubtful. Finally she stood, put down her brush, turned and walked a deliberate path out of the room, fully aware that Inez was observing her every feature and would be expecting her back tomorrow. For some next step.

Elaine did not sleep well that night, tossing and turning, drifting from one troubled dream to another. She got out of bed and tried to read, but some new predicament emerged to the forefront of her awareness and she could find no comfort. She awoke to a moody fatigue. She fussed with her breakfast, was impatient with a nurse, and with pervasive irritation walked into art therapy. She began to work in strong shades and forms of red, contrasting with swaths of black. Inez studied her from another table and finally came over and uttered her first words: "Stay with this. Develop what is happening here. Deliver it." Elaine was startled by those strong words, spoken with such certainty. Deliver it? You deliver a baby. You break open and let this new aliveness come out of you, out into the world which may or may not accept it. On Elaine's canvas, some yellows and greens emerged in a background, buds and shoots; but the reds and the blacks were battling each other. As the morning wore on the bleeding red prevailed; but then the black oils, featuring a slash of dark purple marginalized the reds. Elaine felt stuck and she called Inez for assistance.

"I don't know what to do?"

"What do you want to do?" Inez's words were carefully chosen.

"I want to resolve this. . . this . . . "

"Conflict?"

Elaine took a deep breath. "You can see that?"

"Of course. And you know it well."

Elaine shuddered. "Oh, yes I do."

Now Inez moved her face even with Elaine and locked her eyes. "Deliver it and give it a name."

Elaine found herself frightened and with great effort broke the commanding gaze. Then after another deep breath "Don't you think we should stop?"

Inez spoke gently. "No. Oh, you can try to stop, but it will never work."

Elaine looked back to the canvas, studying it. Finally "It is so obvious. Blood. Earth. Warfare. Life and death. Love and hate. Light and darkness. The battle. Obliterating the seeds of life back here."

Inez nodded.

Elaine felt nauseous, some dark obstruction within her increasing in mass with every deep breath. Her words were a plea to Inez. "This is not helpful."

Inez nodded again. "It is painfully difficult." A pause. "I know what you have been through; now I can see what you are going through."

Elaine noticed that she was digging her fingernails into her palms. She immediately pulled her hands together, then observed that she looked as if she were praying. Her vulnerability framed her words. "I need to resolve this."

After a long, reflective pause Inez spoke. "Resolve is an unrealistic word. These are the polarities of your life. They are mine also. We must learn to face them with courage and wisdom."

Elaine was bewildered. "I really don't know what you are talking about."

"I know. Take this with you to your sleep. Tomorrow we will discuss it further."

That night was heavy, an endless shuffling of concerns and fears. She could see her painting project in her mind, in detail, and it would evolve even more tomorrow. Inner doors were somehow opening whether she liked it or not, a dreadful sense of loss of control.

She arose early, got a cup of tea with the night nurse, and went to the day room and sat by the window to watch the sunrise. A day like any other day was beginning, filled with routines for many people out there. But here in this search for meaning, all routines were challenged. They had provided a kind of numbing safety. She longed for their return.

She picked at breakfast, eating at a table alone. Arriving late for group therapy she slipped into an edge of the group without her usual attention to what was happening with others. Group members noticed her lack of presence but did not engage her partly because they were preoccupied with a role-play to experience the deep guilt one of the young men felt regarding what he had done to his brother. She watched the clock, waiting for art therapy to begin at 10:30.

Inez had come early, moved the easel over to a corner, with two chairs in front of the painting. Elaine found her meditating as she approached and sat down quietly, respecting the silence. Elaine, once again, entered into her painting, touching it with her thoughts, imaging its skin, its inner heart, its flow, its unpredictable volatility. She was searching for a metaphor so as to name it when Inez nodded, sighed and spoke.

"Think of archetypes. Ancient wisdom. Raw truth."

Elaine was in a high degree of alertness, open to every nuance of the moment, sensing an energy flowing around her that was at the same time inviting and dangerous. But she could not grasp it.

Inez closed her eyes again, went somewhere for grounding, and finally nodded. "Okay. For instance, make use of the story of the two wolves."

Elaine wondered if she had heard her correctly. Then bewildered. "I really don't know what you are talking about."

"The red wolf and the silver wolf."

Elaine searched her bank of analogies, then shook her head. "Nothing."

Now it was Inez who was puzzled. "This is 1984 and with all your adventurous journeying in your young college life you have not heard of this old parable?"

Elaine shook her head. If there was any other activity in the room Elaine was unaware of it. Her absolute attention was riveted on Inez.

"Very well, I will tell you. This is an old story. It is common to speak of it as coming from the Cherokee tradition. But my grandfather, who introduced it to me when I was a little girl, insisted it belonged to the Lakota Sioux wisdom. He had traveled there early in his life and discovered it.

But whatever. It seems that one time there was a fierce skirmish of one tribe with another. It lasted a full day, in small hills, and it was bloody. Many of the braves were hurt and three were killed. The village mourned, then took counsel for wisdom. Two young boys observed all these things. They were frightened with the violence and perplexed with the mystery. Why did this have to occur? What was to be gained? There was land enough and game enough for all.

They mustered their courage and approached Grandfather. They asked him directly: 'Why do men fight each other in this manner?'

Grandfather looked at them carefully, a look that reached across many years, even across ages. And he told them. 'Within the chests of all of us there live two wolves: a red wolf and a silver wolf. The red wolf is frightful. Dark red-rust coat and deep black eyes. He is fierce. He is jealous, never wants to share and will take what he wants. He is angry. He never forgets an insult or an offense and wants revenge. He will search and destroy, killing if necessary. He is powerful. Then there is the silver wolf. He is very strong but kind with deep blue eyes. He is faithful to his friendships. He protects. He loves beauty, enjoys the wind and sky and the waters. He desires peace and the red wolf hates him for it. So they are continually at war.'

The eyes of the young boys were open wide in both amazement and fear. 'Grandfather, do these wolves live in your chest?'

'Oh yes. They have been fighting on and off all of my life.'

Then they asked hesitantly. 'And do they live in our chests?'

'Oh yes. The older you get the more you will become familiar with their fight.'

The boys pondered this truth. Then one of them asked in a small voice: 'But grandfather, which one of them will win?'

Grandfather waited for a moment so that they would clearly understand. 'The one that wins is the one you feed.'"

Inez looked away in a slightly weary expression. The story was obviously hers as well as Elaine's.

Elaine moved close to the painting, studied if from another angle, then turned to Inez. "That story came to mind as you looked at this?"

Inez looked up. Then she looked away, far away, as if she were re-visiting a very old place in time. All was still for a minute. Finally she stood, captured Elaine with a command of her eyes, then broke the connection, turned and walked away.

* * *

"Sounds as if your psychology class is stimulating a lot of memories."

"Yeah. The whole theme about what really restores health. Not just fixing something but genuine turning points."

Dr. Keith mused. "It is interesting that this all comes back in a flood after, well, three months now. You had mentioned those relationships in the hospital but only in passing. Or so it seemed."

"I think it has taken a while but I am just now getting things in perspective. I am telling you, and no put-down to your profession, but some of the real healers are persons so human, so genuine, that they enlighten. Relationships. The word always sounded a bit trivial to me."

"And the story of the wolves. You referred to that only once or twice at the time. Now it is there for you as a kind of core insight."

Elaine carefully explored his words before responding. "I didn't get it at first. Oh, it is a dramatic story, and pretty relevant to that painting. That projection of my inner conflict. But it sounded too simple, like 'Make love, not war.' Easy to say, hard to do. More to it than that."

"But now it is there, kind of at the center of your attention, active in your decisions and interpretations."

"Yeah. I think it has been operating without my knowing it."

"How do you mean?"

"Well, let's see. Okay. When I was in the hospital Brian called most every day. At first I welcomed every one. But he could not offer particularly good counsel. Actually he has always been such a hard-headed realist that he can come across as a total pessimist. But it is much worse now. He lives with pain and his increasing limitations. I will need to send him money every month. But I am having to step back from his bitterness and his dark place. His silver wolf is not prevailing.

And then there is mother. Her cards, letters, and calls I generally rejected. I saw them as toxic and harmful to me. And I became aware that it would be equally toxic if I wanted to expose her hypocrisy, her craziness and cruelty. To reveal it to the family. Something said it was not wise to do that. I started to back away. As a result, once I was out of the hospital I could go back to Gary and visit people, including mother. Whenever they would try to pull out of me what I had gone through I deflected it. It was not repression as you say. Just not feeding the red wolf."

"And then all of the new energy you started giving to Ellen. That was very positive, filled with hope for a new start."

She sighed. "Yes. It hurts to think of all she went through this last year. I saw her getting more and more depressed, getting fatter because she would eat when nothing but her sadness and turmoil was coming from me. I knew I had to move her away from all that darkness. And I think we turned a corner."

"How did you do that?"

"I just finally realized that she wanted so much to interact with me more. I remember a simple time when I was giving her a bath. Her hair was wet and soapy so I pulled it up to a point, and held up the mirror so she could see. She broke out laughing and soon we were both splashing in the bubbles. So simple and obvious. Then when I began to read to her again she would snuggle, sometimes excited by the stories, sometimes almost fearful.

"Really encouraging focus. Sounds like you are on track."

Elaine sighed, then held up crossed fingers.

There followed a long pause. "So, now I want to go back to your wolves. I am interested in your insight at this juncture. It seems very important."

"Say more."

"Well, it reveals your personal experience with both components. Good and evil. Love and hate. Life and death. The full range of human nature. Too often people don't have the courage to face that life is fundamentally conflictual. Oh, they will admit it in theory but will otherwise make a morality play out of it. Good conquers evil. Justice will eventually prevail. It is too hard to admit to the full ongoing reality of existence."

Her voice was edged with sarcasm. "You mean nice guys don't finish first? Sorry, but you are lecturing."

"Hmm. I really don't mean to. It's just – well this is not theoretical for you. Let's see. Okay, go back and remember the cascade of events before you had to be hospitalized. And remember specifically your honest, vivid description of how you would really like to get even with the killer. Skin him alive. Dismember him. Remember."

Elaine was silent, warding off a wave of numbness. "Oh yes."

"You see, what you call your red wolf was fully alive in you in that moment. You claimed it, then wanted to discredit yourself for having such feelings. Saying you were no different than the killer. I tried to hold you to your experience, that this was a genuine part of you, a potential for real health and recovery. Had you denied this, repressed it, not faced it, it could easily have prevailed against your silver wolf which was seeking to emerge."

Elaine put her head back on the chair pillow and closed her eyes. She imagined the wolves in her in that moment. The red one had receded to the edge, but he snarled, lips pulled back to reveal sharp teeth, eyes aglow. The silver one had increased in stature. He was lying in soft grass, in the cool shade, vigilant and determined but gentle and peaceful. And so very strong. Then she remembered: "The one you feed is the one that prevails."

She sat up and turned to Dr. Keith. "Thank you. Thank you for insisting I claim the full measure. Look the devil in the eye as it were, and calculate the stakes." After a pause she continued. "What comes to mind right now is a promise of my religion: 'You shall know the truth, and the truth shall make you free.' "

Dr. Keith would usually deflect any issues of religion, referring them to her priest. But now he was deeply touched by these words. "I must say that I place everything on that principle. I could not otherwise do this work."

* * *

Being back in class at Illinois-Chicago full time was itself restorative. Especially in brisk autumn, and she imagined as she looked around the classroom how many of those students, like herself, simply equated the slow emergence of leafy golds and reds with the stoic energy and resolve for still another school year. So it had been for seventeen Septembers since kindergarten.

And this advanced psychology class had launched into immediate relevance. The discussion centered on factors which contribute to therapeutic progress, or resolution, or even healing. The pre-requisite had been a class addressing diagnostic criteria and classification of mental disorders – how to name the demons. Now the focus was on how to exorcise them.

Elaine listened carefully and took good notes on the various types of treatment procedures in clinical practice. There was always the unbraiding of twisted social histories, theories of family dynamics (if they only knew of hers!), numerous behavioral strategies, neuro-psychological treatment, cognitive reprogramming, eliciting insight, support and nurturance, relationship therapy, and, of course, always the older psychoanalytic emphases on interpreting material being revealed from the Unconscious. Elaine carefully tested every category through the prisms of her therapy and particularly regarding her own hospitalization just five months ago. She was feeling so much better now, stronger, on track, centered, many of the parts of her coming back together in a flow of new confidence. There were the abrupt setbacks appearing without warning: the dreaded night terrors which would launch her thrashing and being unable to scream, or the jolting reflex at the sudden sight of a man in the shadows across the street. But still the bleak downward spiral had dissipated.

The class was turning its attention to the psychology of religion, specifically in America. The professor's challenge was to analyze the psycho-social effects of religious movements during the evolution of the nation, particularly those which emphasized mankind's fallen state and need for salvation. A two-page handout included a summary of the Great Awakening in early America, a frightening and frenzied revival which swept the countryside. Some preacher named

Jonathan Edwards had a sermon called *Sinners in the Hands of an Angry God* which terrified thousands, leading them down to the altar to be "saved." But saved from what? Hellfire and brimstone? That seemed to be a primitive doctrine, contradicting any notion of a loving God. Saved from evil forces? But those forces are composed of other human beings. Saved from one's own self, from one's own passions and blindness and even loss of sanity? That suggested that life is fragile with no hope for stability.

Elaine reflected on her own Catholic heritage. The parochial schools were, for the most part, somewhat miserable. She recalled one school in the third grade which she really liked. The nuns there were different; they would play jump rope with the kids. And the principal was good-natured and would sometimes playfully pull her pony tail. Here was precious and trusted affection from a male which was so new for her. But otherwise it was a drag. Most of the nuns were severe in their seriousness, punitive in their management of students. Mass was a routine, and periodic confession was mechanical. But they did succeed in implanting a fundamental program which followed her to this day. She could hear the voice of the nuns saying it, again and again: "In life you get exactly what you deserve." And Todd did not deserve the mistake of loving her.

She refocused on the professor who was talking about the Protestant practice of the "altar call," the parade of penitents down to the altar to be purged of their sinfulness. To be saved. From the colonial evangelists down through large mainline churches in the Bible Belt and up to the latest Billy Graham crusade, they came as deeply troubled persons concerned for their very souls. The class was asked to put aside all presumptions, to imagine that they were visitors from another galaxy sent on a scientific expedition to analyze human social behavior. Now they were studying this religious quest for redemption. And Elaine's attention arrested as the professor read one of the stanzas of an "altar call" hymn. The words might have been written for her:

6. TRANSFORMATION

Just as I am though tossed about
With many a conflict, many a doubt,
Fightings within and fears without
O Lamb of God, I come, I come.

The description was of her own self, her identity, the turbulence of her inner world. The reference to "many" conflicts and doubts seemed understated. But the words that leaped out were "fightings within and fears without."

There it was. The "fightings within" took her immediately to the metaphor of the two wolves. And what provoked their continuous conflict were the "fears without." It was always not far from her mind: He was out there. But where? Doing what? Was he still mindful of her? Was he wanting to find her? And Ellen?

To these fears the red wolf would arouse her to a continual vigilance. It prompted her to contact the detectives once again, and they were hardly calming. They were sure who he was, sure of the general neighborhood where he moved about. They considered him to be a monster and they hated their lack of evidence to bring him in. And then that day when, frustrated by their helplessness, they had made that remark which would forever shock her. It was uttered almost offhand: "We will deny we said this, but if you ever decided to have someone take him out, we would look the other way."

Now the red wolf was provoked. The possibility of striking back, of annihilating him with one decision, of imagining him with his face blown away. Closure. Justice. Her controlled rage left a metallic taste in her mouth, and she relished it.

But soon the silver wolf appeared with his dire warning. Be assured: if she ventured on such revenge it could devour her instead. She would return to that session with Dr. Keith where she owned the full truth, that nothing on earth would be more satisfying to her than to skin him alive, to dismember him. And with these thoughts came the horror that she could be just as hideously primitive and grotesque as he was.

She slipped out of class before it ended, overcome by crosscurrents of nausea, confusion, weakness, and above all feeling that she and her life were haunted. The words to the old hymn kept returning, about being tossed about by conflicts and doubts. But the one phrase repeated itself over and over again: *fightings within and fears without, O Lamb of God I come.*

But what did that mean: come to the Lamb of God? She had only a distant idea. Her church had always increased her sense of guilt: that if she were in despair it was because she deserved it. But these words promised some kind of rescue. How? She thought of Imogene who could explain concepts out of some ancient wisdom. But Imogene was at the hospital and Elaine never wanted to go back there again. She thought of an urgent appointment with Dr. Keith, but on the subject of God or religion he had repeatedly backed away. And then she thought of Inez who would not judge her for wanting to get revenge, but who took her to the big picture where there was hope for escape. Suddenly she could see Inez's face and on that face the unmistakable message, the vital truth, words that were to become a mantra for all the days ahead. *You must feed the silver wolf. Feed the silver wolf. Feed the silver wolf.*

* * *

It had been ten days since her appointment with Dr. Keith, but Elaine had been obsessed with a remark she had made about Ellen. It was like a forgotten melody that had suddenly returned and played again and again in her head. She could even hear the echo of her own words in the office: "I had to move her away from all that darkness."

She searched through her notebook for the name of the child psychologist Dr. Keith had recommended back during her hospitalization. Now she sat in his waiting room in the suburban office building offset from the busy traffic. His was a corner office, tucked privately among the well-groomed maple trees and the carpeted lawn. The setting made for a cloistered effect, quiet and anonymous. She thought perhaps it might be a soothing place for children. She walked over to one of his framed credentials and studied it. Matthew McQuistion, Ph.D. University of Michigan, 1980. Post-Doctoral Residency, University of Florida, 1981. What could he do for Ellen that she could not do? Maybe a lot she hoped.

Precisely at the appointed time the door opened. "Elaine Atkinson?" She nodded. "Matt McQuistion. Please come in."

Elaine immediately noted that he was "Matt." A bit less formal than Dr. Keith. Maybe too informal, too smooth. How does one know? Would he be "Dr. Matt" to his children patients?

She had completed a two-page medical/social history checklist, and while he read it she assessed him further. First his beard which was neatly trimmed, a bit of an exclamation point to his face. But groomed and not reactionary. Not likely that he smoked pot. His face seemed kind and she sensed an ease and patience in him. He was slightly less in stature than Dr. Keith. Then a sudden association: he had a slight resemblance to Todd! That produced a wave of discomfort and she immediately looked away from him to the details of his office. She saw the table in the corner with small toys, animals, and designs. For the children to explore while he watched she guessed. The choice of a sofa or three chairs. A jar of what looked like peppermint rounds on his desk. Pavlov rewarding the little dogs? And then the pictures on the wall, the lake and sailboat, the carrousel in a park.

"I see that you are a widow" he said, interrupting her office survey.

"Yes."

"Your daughter's father?"

Elaine frowned slightly, sensing something indecent in the question. "Yes, Ellen was conceived four years ago. He died shortly after."

The doctor looked up, waiting for the obvious explanation.

"Her father was killed by an intruder in our home." There, she thought. Let's put it all on the table.

To her surprise he did not pursue more details. She assumed that he would return to that later. Instead he asked "So what brings you to my office?"

Elaine paused. He is wanting to know if this is about me or Ellen. A good question. But I have my own therapist and don't need another.

"I see Dr. Keith made the referral. Are you in treatment with him?"

"Yes."

"Can you summarize what that is about?"

She sighed. "I suffered serious post-traumatic stress after Todd, my husband, was murdered. It happened in front of me. He also critically wounded my brother who was visiting. He got away and is still out there."

The doctor was taken aback by the sudden intensity in the room. He folded his hands on his chest and waited for the next cue to emerge. To Elaine it looked like he was quietly praying, and she found some strange reassurance in this. She could then continue.

"I can almost read what Dr. Keith will report to you when I authorize release of information. 'Elaine's pregnancy was characterized by powerful ambivalent swings. On the one hand she wanted her daughter to live and blossom as a remnant of her husband would live on. And she might well have committed suicide except for being pregnant. On the other hand she questioned why her daughter should have to come into a world so evil.' Actually Dr. Keith would have phrased the issues more clinically."

"But that would be the essence of his report."

"Yes."

"And this year you want me to work with your daughter. Because . . . "

"Because she has gone through really bad stuff. She needs someone to help her put the pieces back together."

The pause was awkward. Elaine knew that he needed to hear a lot more of narrative, descriptions of Ellen during the last three turbulent years. But where to begin? What to emphasize, what to summarize, what to let him discover? And any discussion of what Ellen must have been experiencing only served to exacerbate Elaine's deep sense of inadequacy.

Finally the doctor spoke. "If there were chapters to Ellen's story, what, in a few words, would each of those chapters be about?"

This was helpful. It gave Elaine a structure. She could depict just the scenarios, the big picture, and he could fill in the details. He could learn what more he needed from either her or Ellen.

"Okay. Chapter One. The pregnancy. This new life in my uterus is truly my only reason for continuing to live. But I am constantly stressed. I don't eat or sleep much. I don't drink or take meds for her sake. But I am lost, living in fear, talking only to the cat. How much of that darkness seeped through to her?

Then Chapter Two. Her actual birth. Early medical fears that she might not even survive, and if so with what kind of major deficits. But she made it out into neo-natal intensive care. Let me authorize you to get all those records. Initially she would not thrive. She rejected the breast; maybe fear and stress were souring my milk. And then it would take most of a day for me to get one bottle feeding into her.

Chapter Three. She changes from being emaciated to being chubby, wanting to eat all the time. With Dr. Keith we talked about her finding food as a substitute for love and nurture. That made me want to hold her even closer. But the fears increased dramatically when the killer found out where I lived. I grabbed her and a few things and fled the city.

Chapter Four is hard for me to describe. She was a sweet child and looked for reasons to laugh. I remember one time when I was feeding her. She was studying my face and with that curious, intent look put her finger in my mouth. I started sucking on her finger, just as she was sucking on the bottle. She stopped, I gestured toward her bottle, then back to her finger, and she laughed. Her first joke. She got it.

And yet so much of the time she had to endure my depression. I was failing as a mother: feeling wholly inadequate, helpless. I hired a nanny, Carolyn, to help me so I could return to school. Ellen seemed to respond well with her and then she adapted to the more depressing times with me.

Chapter Five was my hospitalization. I managed to stop a deadly downward spiral, but in my insights I became aware of just how much darkness Ellen had been living in. I vowed to bring some light back into her world. And to keep that vow I will need your help. How soon can you see her?"

And so it was done. The forms completed, the rules explained, the appointment made. As Elaine walked out of the office building, she experienced vivid clarity in all her senses. The smell of what must be a recently cut lawn. A silken breeze across her face and arms. The quietness of a place forming a background for sounds of insects flying, and one bird on the wing. And the light of bright day, flooding the afternoon sky, carving sharp shadows in its challenge to the darkness.

* * *

First it caught her by surprise, without warning. Then it struck and she was seized by a bolt of fear. On the bulletin board of the administration building were the list of all students organized by their declared majors. And under the category entitled Biology and Chemistry was her name: Elaine Atkinson. There for the entire world to read! After all her efforts to have her phone and mailboxes unlisted, here all anonymity was blown and thousands of students could access her.

She would have torn the list down instantly, even in front of other students who were examining it. But it was behind a locked glass cover. She felt frozen, momentarily unable to move, sensing that other students were aware of something wrong in her. Her mind raced to find a focus, any kind of focus. What to do? Then she followed an impulse and went immediately into the administration building to lodge her protest and to have her name taken off that public list.

The room felt chaotic, buzzing with secretaries and telephones, consultations and conferences, computers and copy machines, and persons coming and going from small offices to file rooms. She paused, took a deep breath, determined to steady herself. Scanning the large room her eyes returned twice to woman working behind what looked to be a long registration counter. Something about her seemed safe. Perhaps the early grey hair of middle age honestly claimed and not hidden. Her quiet demeanor, calm in this storm. An easy and reassuring smile to what appeared to be a confused student.

Elaine waited until this woman completed her work with the student, then quickly moved to her. "I must talk with you immediately."

The woman looked up and slowly engaged her facility for careful and precise inspection. She had, over the years, encountered students in every conceivable state of mind: frightened, angry, frustrated, confused, sad, defeated, and some determined, proud, hopeful, confident. But here was an intensity that required more clarification.

"I am Mrs. Clark. Sylvia Clark. How may I help you?"

Elaine started to speak but could not find the words. She felt immobilized. Like a statue. Where to begin? How to summarize her vital need for anonymity? What to say?

"Just take a moment if you need." The words from Ms. Clark were soothing in their patience.

The past three years had been a proving ground for Elaine to learn ways of grounding herself in the midst of chaos. She took another deep breath, surveyed her place at the counter and the nearness of other students, and claimed her intuitive trust of Ms. Clark.

"This is very personal and private. Could we maybe meet at that desk over there?"

A brief silence followed, allowing Ms. Clark to broaden her assessment. "Here at the counter we seek quick clarification of curriculum problems. If you need an appointment for a more comprehensive issue . . . "

"No! I don't think that will be necessary. Maybe you can quickly help." Elaine paused, searching for words of simple solution for a complex issue. "For reasons that I cannot go into here, legal reasons, medical reasons, I require privacy. I cannot have my name listed in public places. And I find that it is listed out there on that bulletin board where persons have declared their majors in chemistry and biology."

Ms. Clark studied Elaine and the problem she posed. Finally she replied: "This is most unusual. Let me think. We certainly do honor requests for privacy of student grades, health records, and, yes, legal issues. Hmm." She looked around, first to one small office then to another. "I see Mrs. Dunbar might be free in a minute of two. She is in a brief conference just now. Maybe you can explain your need to her."

"Thank you so much. But. . . but do you think you could go out there just now and white out my name on that list?"

"We will look into that shortly. Stay here and let me see if Mrs. Dunbar is free right now."

Things moved rather quickly in the hour that followed. Elaine appreciated how these two women could extract just enough of her story to legitimatize her need for anonymity, but, at the same time, did not pursue unnecessary details. A call to Dr. Keith was returned and he provided the medical order to authorize restrictions on any public use of Elaine's name. Mrs. Dunbar discovered that there was precedent for the university to issue a pseudonym for Elaine on all information and communications within the university. Henceforth she would be the student known as Eleanor Kehrberg, her grandmother's maiden name. This practice would prevail throughout her remaining studies at Illinois-Chicago.

Elaine was deeply touched by the care of these women, and so impressed with their skill at solving the problem. She fumbled her attempt to express her appreciation but they simply smiled. "Our pleasure to help you Eleanor." And as she walked out of the office she could not resist going to the bulletin board to check the lists. And already her name had been covered with white-out.

* * *

"But don't you see. In having my name changed at school I fed the red wolf! I caved in to my fears. That makes the red wolf stronger."

Dr. Keith made no attempt to disguise his frown. "No, I don't see that at all. Your fears are natural, healthy defenses. At least on this matter. Do you really believe that it would have been more mature of you to just 'tough it out', or to move into denial, acting like that man is really not out there?"

Now it was Elaine's fierce glare that could not be restrained. She breathed deeply, then rubbed her eyes and blanketed her face in her hands. Time seemed suspended.

He carefully broke the silence. "Talk about what is happening right now."

"It is not that simple."

"But give it form. Give it life outside of you. You know. . . on the one hand, then on the other."

"O.K. You say it was healthy of me to claim my fears, to protect myself. Nice, easy clinical interpretation. Can't you see that inside me it is a return to the old feelings, so familiar: scared to death, hiding from him, house-bound, running away. Don't you understand how hard I have worked to get beyond that? And now here I am again, a timid student ducking around all the corners of the campus. Eleanor Kehrberg! I might as well have a rubber nose and wig. I hate this."

"Now, do it the other way. Stroll around campus introducing yourself as Elaine Atkinson. Go back to that psychology class which stimulated so many insights and decisions within you, and disclose your experience to the professor and your fellow students. How does that feel?"

It was, of course, a rhetorical question. Elaine had to admit that such false bravado would not only expose her to grim possibilities but also would put Ellen in grave danger. It left her feeling horribly depressed, trapped in a life of being forever vigilant.

"Elaine, it is not likely to be forever. I am quite surprised he is still alive or at least not in prison. But even if he were out of the picture, there is only limited safety in life."

"You mean you are as paranoid as I am?"

"Once again you are not paranoid. The peril is real. And I do not face that kind of direct threat. But, yes, I am guarded. We have to be. We take calculated chances in life. And we give ultimate trust to very few others."

"Ultimate trust? What kind of a dream world is that?" Elaine stood up and began to pace the room, concentrating on this mystery. "Calculated chances in life" as he put it. So who could she trust, really? No one "ultimately." It seemed as if she had known that only with Todd. Dr. Keith? Yes, he would never hurt her. And he had been there for her through the most difficult of times. But he went home at night and lived elsewhere between appointments.

But who else? "Calculated chances." Well there was the psychology professor, Dr. Schneider, whom she sensed was non-judgmental, sincere, finding true satisfaction when his students were stimulated by their explorations. He seemed genuinely kind. Kindness could be blended with strength. She had met strong and determined people who still, by nature, would not want to see others suffer. And the faces of some of her fellow students passed before her. McKenzie. Jeri. Walter. And Carolyn. Of course, Carolyn.

"You seem in deep thought?"

Elaine continued to look out the window, across the campus, as she answered him. "Something about what you said. 'Calculated chances.' It made me think how much energy I have given to vigilance. Always scanning for the red wolf. But I am not taking any chances with people who seem basically kind. Kindness. I have too often dismissed it as soft and weak. But it is out there. I found it in a gentle nurse at the hospital. In a thoughtful, considerate clerk over at administration. In the hopes of some of those students who aspire to be public school teachers."

She turned, then, facing her doctor, carefully shaping the very thought that was coming out of her mouth as a pronouncement. "If I set about scanning for kind-heartedness, believing in it, then I start feeding the silver wolf."

* * *

It took a while for her to grow into the name of Eleanor Kehrberg. In the early weeks after introducing herself to new classmates she would sometimes just keep walking when someone called out her name. This left the impression with some that she was either aloof, totally pre-occupied or a bit crazy. And she had to explain to Dr. Schneider that her name had been changed for some complex legal and genealogical reasons. She smiled: "It's just a long story. Maybe sometime we can analyze it psychologically."

Coursework had become truly invigorating. She was besieged by stimulation coming from seemingly every direction. Once it reminded her of the weekend she and Todd spent at a health spa. There she had discovered an enclosed private shower with a large round nozzle spreading its gentle cascade down from above while six other nozzles engaged her body from unique angles. So were the challenges of school brisk and revitalizing. She had forgotten how biology and chemistry had actually been a source of pleasure in high school, and she returned to them now as a double major, restoring her confidence and her emerging purpose. And she seized every psychology class which fit her schedule, searching for insights to explain cruelty and madness.

And she was making new friends, at least prospects for "the calculated chance of trust." They found her to be spirited, affable, but also mysterious. She was six to eight years older than some of them and they wondered who she was, how she had just suddenly materialized on campus, how she could be so accomplished as a student, what she had been doing before deciding to go to college. Elaine could immediately detect the most subtle probe of inquiry and had become adept at deflecting it. And after all a little mystery was an alluring feature in an older co-ed. But some would be more direct in their curiosity and this was a bit awkward. She wanted to be open and engaging, but she also wanted to build a shield around the last five years of her life. She was not repressing it; her therapy was engineered to enable her to face it. But it would take more of what Dr. Keith had called ultimate trust to disclose her experience to these new acquaintances. And she shuddered to imagine what any of them would do to her revelation of the reality that "he is still out there." Their horror would, in and of itself, activate a new web of fear. More food for the red wolf.

* * *

Elaine would later remember the day she spotted Dr. Kempers walking across the commons. She was not aware of being in any conscious zone of scanning for kind people. But when he appeared out of the past onto that sidewalk, her thoughts emerged in an instant of focus: could there possibly be a more genuine manifestation of trust than this man?

When Todd was in dental school, Elaine had worked over at Rush University Medical Center. She had secretarial duties of collating materials, tracking student records, coordinating the interface between clinical and academic activities. It was there she had met Dr. Forrest Kempers, Academic Dean. He was a quiet man, without pretension, an introvert such that the passing world would never dream that he was an esteemed scientist and an administrator known nationally for setting the very highest standards of medical education. And for reasons that were unclear he felt comfortable with Elaine and increasingly interested in her own new future. One day in a conversation about college life she sheepishly admitted that she had bungled her first year of college, choosing the life of parties and alcohol over books; and by the second year her self-esteem had plummeted to a low point and she dropped out. She chose to work to support Todd in dental school. It was in that conversation, touched by this man's sincerity, that she asked him. "Did I ruin my chances? If I came back and really plunged into science, would it be possible for me to be re-admitted?" He thought for only a moment when he had answered: "My goodness, of course. There is no reason why the first irrational and impulsive years of college should destroy your life. If you have truly changed your ways, then go for it. Make it your turning point."

That memory triggered an impulse to run out and greet him on the sidewalk. But quickly she saw the folly of that. He would no doubt be headed for a next appointment and could not stop and talk. And talk about what? And how embarrassing it would be if he did not even remember her. And why not? It had been almost four years.

But as he disappeared around the corner she had a strong feeling of having been suddenly blessed. Running into Dean Kempers was such a serendipity, a stunning moment when she sensed doors opening which had long been closed and pathways into a future slowly illuminating. And it was reasonable that he would remember her. When she returned to work after Todd was killed, staff members were awkward in their conflicted attempts to both reach out to her and to give her distance. But it was apparent that word had gone out from administration that Elaine was to be given the space she needed, and the kindness and respect she always felt from the dean made it clear where the order originated. And when she finally felt the need to resign her work, to just walk away, it was he who asked to see her for a few minutes, and with absolute sincerity conveyed to her that if she ever wanted to return she would have his personal welcome.

And so a plan began to evolve. She needed to see him, to consult with him. She was not at all sure what she would say or expect of him, but she had an almost surreal confidence that their meeting would bring clarity to her, both in her current decisions and to her unfolding future. So certain was she of the value of their meeting that she deliberately avoiding having any agenda. There was just something about Dr. Kempers that she believed would elicit from her what had been clouded or hidden.

She would go see him at his office.

* * *

How well Elaine remembered the routines of the dean. He always, without fail, arrived at his office no later than 6:30 A.M, long before others. He made the coffee, checked for messages, and then closed his door to be about his paperwork. Elaine knew of the basement entrance into the medical school, then the passage to the print shop and the back elevator to administration. She carried a stack of old folders to look like staff in the event she were noticed by security. But the hallway was empty and, just as she suspected, his routine had not changed in five years. All lights were on in the reception area and she noted with a smile the red light on the coffee maker.

After stopping for a deep breath, she tapped on his door, then opened it slightly, peeking inside.

"Hello in there. Just like old times."

Dr. Kempers turned in his swivel chair, adjusted his glasses so as to look twice, then stood up slowly. "Elaine? Elaine, is that you?"

Her smile conveyed a depth of sweetness she had all but forgotten. "Dear Dr. Kempers! I didn't know if you would remember me or not."

"Elaine it is really you! My goodness, what an extraordinary surprise." He paused to bring all of his faculties to focus. "What do you mean would I remember you? Of course. How could I forget? Just look at you."

"And look at you. Your distinction increases with every year."

He laughed. "And what does that mean? Some euphemism for 'older and more grey but passable.'"

"It has only been four years."

The dean was touched by the kindness of the gentle face before him, bringing flashbacks to the same haunted face when he last looked upon it. He immediately offered her coffee. Elaine emphasized that she did not want to intrude and he assured her that anything on his agenda could be temporarily postponed.

They began with his brief summary of life in the medical school office since her departure, and some of the names led to reminiscences of better times. Then came the awkward moment when Dr. Kempers alluded to the tragedy, its horrific impact upon him and others, and the perpetual concern for Elaine. In the silence that followed Elaine was uncertain as what to relate about her last five years. She spoke in general terms with a considered objectivity, sounding, she once thought with amusement, like Dr. Keith might sound if he were briefly encapsulating her case. She referenced her flight from Chicago, her hyper-vigilant return, her psychotherapy, her concern for Ellen, her hospitalization, and then her resolve to move forward and put the terror behind her. And this, of course, led to her return to Illinois-Chicago as a student.

"That's impressive Elaine. Back in school again. I remember a conversation we had when Todd was still finishing school in which you expressed that ambition."

She all but interrupted him in her excitement. "Do you really? That's amazing! That full conversation all came back to me earlier this week." She was momentarily silent, considering it. "Just amazing."

"So. How is it going? What is your major, your goal?"

And suddenly there was no easy response. She was not confused; the logic of this transition was to be expected. But whenever she imagined meeting the dean, if that were even possible, and she anticipated such a question, she had deliberately put it aside. She did not want to create an agenda which closed off dialogue with him. She did not want to present him with a plan to hopefully approve. She wanted his input. But now the question was on their table. It was followed by a full minute of silence. "Well, that is a tough one to answer. I am majoring in biology and chemistry. As for my goal . . . "

It was then that Elaine knew why she had wanted this specific conversation with the dean. The thought had crossed her mind several times but she discounted it. And now, in spite of herself, she heard the words spilling out. "Dean Kempers, do you think it would ever be possible, I mean with the low g.p.a of my freshman year, do you think a person could ever be admitted to your medical school? Remember I used to score the placement applications for medical school. I saw all those that had been rejected. Is it possible that I could ever be considered?"

The dean studied her carefully. It was immediately apparent that she was not here to manipulate special favors lodged in their history. And he saw that she had not even rehearsed this response. He was hearing the sounds of an emerging dream.

Now he required the period of silence, shaping his response with as much accuracy and honesty as possible. Finally. "It would be most unusual, Elaine, as you know the g.p.a. is a significant factor." He paused again, experiencing a heaviness entering the room. "But yes, such a thing would be possible. Demonstrating excellence in your science studies would certainly elevate the placement profile."

Her hand went to her mouth, as if to stifle whatever random sound was emerging. Then she composed herself. "Oh, that is so much to hear." She reached out to take his hand, to shake it or bless it or for some kind of primal connection. He clasped her hand with both of his.

"But then you have always made your own pathways haven't you." They sat quietly, he looking at her face and lovely hair, she contemplating their joined hands.

Finally he carried forward, sitting back. "But tell me Elaine. Why in the world would you want to become a doctor? Why that? And may I assure you that if you were pursue application to this medical school, the entire admission team would be honing in on your answer to that question." He paused. "Do you have any idea, even at this stage of thought, how you would answer?"

The response she would make resided deep within her. She knew it well but had never expressed it to any other living soul. Not even to Todd. She thought she never would. And now, and now, it would be shared with another.

Her words flowed easily, softly as a song. "I have known since I was six years old that I wanted to be a psychiatrist. I have always known that for sure."

Dr. Kempers was absolutely still. That's all. No more explanation. Her face, voice, and thoughts became a congruent moment which required his most penetrating search. And she sat through the quietness with absolute calmness. Finally he measured his own words.

"That is a remarkable thing for you to say. I don't think I have ever heard anything resembling that. Oh, children will want to be 'the doctor' who is mysterious and highly esteemed. But you say you wanted to be a psychiatrist from age six? And all your life, including down through these mature years, this still holds true? I don't understand."

Now it was Elaine who was the one offering the hope for enlightenment. She spoke as if to comfort the good doctor, to reassure him of the reality of her childhood revelation.

"You see, when I was six, and before that really, I was, shall we say, up a tree, way out on a limb. I knew I was not going to make it if I did not understand more."

"Up a tree. . . way out on a limb. . . can you say more about that."

"I knew I lived in a world where people did really bad things to others. I did not know how to keep going."

"Really bad people doing really bad things to others. . .things you saw or things which happened to you too?"

"Both."

"And you say you knew you were not going to make it . . ."

"Why live any longer? Unless, I thought, I can understand why human beings do what they do. Even those bad things. And I picked up in the family somewhere that there was a doctor called a psychiatrist who could address that question. So, you see, I have always known that I wanted to be a psychiatrist."

7. Commencement

For a change it was Dr. Keith who seemed to be the one searching for a way to make sense out of things. When he shook his head and looked down as if to hide a slight smile, Elaine challenged him.

"You seem amused."

"Oh no. Far from that. Astonished perhaps. Just imagining you strolling into the dean's office at 6:30 A.M., unannounced, and then his giving you audience and such bold counsel. That is a lot to comprehend."

"Why?"

"Well, first of all that is out of character for him. He is always quite friendly, but he is in such demand that people sometimes have to wait weeks to get in that office. His secretary manages his appointment schedule and I have known attempts to bribe her so as to move up on the list."

"I am not surprised."

"Oh. Why is that?"

"Those of us who used to work backstage at administration would frequently interact with him at the coffee counter, at the copy machine, or just in passing. I always found him to be absolutely truthful. No games. The last time I saw him his concern for me was undeniably sincere. And to deflect your suspicion of my active narcissism, it is not that I am so special. He is."

Dr. Keith considered this carefully. "Okay. Point taken. But then there is more. He actually told you that it would be at least possible for you to matriculate in medical school?"

Elaine sighed. "Possible, yes. A long shot."

Dr. Keith smiled. "That is high ambition. And now there is this new central issue, of you wanting to be a psychiatrist. I am taken by surprise, although I must say that your assessment of other mental health workers has always seemed to be precise, that is, the way you appreciate who is genuinely helpful and who is not. So, anyway, say a little more about that."

"There is nothing more to say, really. To repeat, I knew from early on that I would have to be a psychiatrist to make any sense out of the chaos of human life. I just always kept that idea to myself."

"But you never even told me about that early decision."

"I know. But I told you about the details of the chaos, and the suicidal thoughts."

"But not about aspiring to be a psychiatrist."

"True." She stopped to deliberate on this. " Maybe it was too touchy because you are a psychiatrist. You are what I want to be."

"You have wanted to be like me?"

"Sure. But not just because you have a gentrified life, a wife and children, vacations and all of the rest. Beyond that. I want access to depth psychology, to understand and then to know what can be done about emotional suffering and craziness."

Elaine was by now familiar with the way Dr. Keith would sometimes go into a review mode, studying her while he seemed to be bringing before his memory a panorama of their time together. She was at ease with this, trusting the work he was doing, that he truly wanted to understand her. Finally he spoke.

"So psychiatrists are the ones who understand the mysteries of life. Did you think of your priest that way?"

"Nah. The priest did not understand who was insane or why or how to cure them. He was just trying to save you from damnation. The psychiatrist was more, more like a witch doctor."

This brought a wry smile from Dr. Keith. "My bubbling cauldron is in the other room."

Elaine laughed. "Replete with toad tongues and newts and poisoned entrails."

There followed a long moment of mutual reflection. Then: "So you are going to pursue this vision from childhood."

She understood the immense implications of this decision. It was not just a new pursuit but a fundamental core commitment. She would remember her answer: "Oh yes. Now it finally begins."

* * *

Elaine was much older than most of the other students but, as a result, she was spared some of the competitive rivalry, being looked upon as a kind of older and more patient sister. And Ellen was blessed with great fortune. The psychology students on campus ran a child day care program where they eagerly evaluated the children according to Piaget's paradigms. They found Ellen to be fascinating, particularly because she had always lived only with adults and was now for the first time interacting with young peers.

And it was around this time that Ellen asked the direct question. She was playing with a screwdriver and moved toward the wall socket as if to insert it. Elaine intervened:

"Don't do that"

"Why?"

"You could die."

"Like Daddy? Did Daddy die doing this?"

Elaine was caught off guard and quickly searched for a path. "No. No. Ah, he got hurt in the head."

Ellen considered this, then went to a picture of Todd on the bookcase and studied it. "I don't see his head hurt."

"Honey, that picture was taken before he got hurt."

"So how did he get hurt?"

"A gunshot."

"Who was it? Anyone I know?"

"No, a stranger."

"Why?"

"He was robbing us."

"Where?"

"In the old house we moved away from."

"What was his name?"

"I don't know."

"How did he get in?"

"Through the basement window."

"Where was I?"

"You were not born yet."

"Where were you?"

"Right there where it happened."

"Was anyone else there?"

"Uncle Brian. He got shot too, but he lived."

Elaine had been quick to understand Ellen's reaction when the goldfish died. It was legitimate grief and a fish funeral was required. And later a hamster funeral. And Ellen sobbed when a pet rabbit died. But now she froze at her daughter's remarks: "I am looking forward to dying so I can see the rabbit and Daddy."

In slow and measured words Elaine answered: "You are in no hurry to die. Time is not passing where Daddy is. He will see you someday when that time comes."

Elaine thought her words to be too close to the old Catholic idea of limbo which she had always thought to be absurd. But in this moment she was thankful for the metaphor. How else to address this with a child?

* * *

Intense study seemed to swallow up time: weeks and months came and went almost unnoticed. As her senior year approached Elaine applied to Rush and also to six other medical schools. Early in the process she was rejected by one with no explanation. That letter triggered waves of anxiety and when she went for her interview at Rush her confidence was at low ebb. She imagined herself to be a fool for having believed she could position herself so as to be competitive with all the other applicants, none of whom had wasted their first year at college. She was further discouraged to learn that she would be examined by Dr. Geiger, a grey and dour man known for having no flexibility or sense of humor. She steeled herself upon his initial comment: "I don't even know why we are interviewing you." There followed a harsh, foreboding silence. And then a moment she would forever remember. A big smile preceded his rich laugh: "Why should we interview you when we all know you so well? Welcome aboard! As soon as you graduate you will be one of the 150 beginning your medical studies."

The numbness was pervasive as she left the office, turned the wrong way down the hall, and finally found herself sitting on a campus bench near a sidewalk. She tried to reconstruct what had just happened, but could only vaguely remember a clumsy "thank you" in a flat and mechanical voice. It seemed so unreal. But it was true; she had actually been accepted into medical school, and right here at Rush. All that hard work, all of the optimism which she had force fed herself, all resulting in a once distant dream now come to fruition. She had the opportunity to be a doctor, carrying forward and deepening the biology she had always enjoyed, and the chemistry, and the creativity, and the exploration of mystery. To re-invent herself now for a new life in a reality beyond her imagination.

The joy swelled. She had no one immediately available that she could tell, no one who would comprehend and embrace this opening to a vast future. She tried to remember if she had ever known this kind of elation, and she found no precedent. Her wedding was memorable but marked by family tensions. The realization that she was pregnant brought tears of happiness but also fears. Ellen's birth had seemed to take place in the middle of a combat zone. And everything else had been swimming into a strong current with only periodic eddies of comfort. No one to hug in this moment, no one to share her dancing spirit. So she would embrace herself, go home, prepare a simple meal for the two of them and have her own glass of wine. Later that night she snuggled close to Ellen, her soft smile responding to her visions of new possibilities so intense that the darkness seemed to be illuminated.

And just as quickly was her elation smothered by a sudden blanket of dread. It happened with no warning. The prospect of graduation after the next semester required Elaine to have a conference with Ms. Clark in administration for a final review of degree requirements and protocol. It was there in the midst of validating coursework and completing forms that Ms. Clark said, rather casually.

"Oh by the way, your use of the pseudonym Eleanor Kehrberg comes to an end. As you walk across the stage the Dean will read the name on your diploma, Elaine Atkinson, and present it to you."

Elaine looked up, stunned, then shaking her head. "Oh no. We can't do that."

Ms. Clark smiled. "Elaine we have no choice. There have been a few other times students have posted their work under a pseudonym, not many but a few, and for a variety of reasons. But at graduation we have to return to accuracy. This is a legal document and even the spelling has to be double-checked."

Elaine could hardly move as the fear expanded into alarm, then the beginnings of panic. She took a deep breath. "Wait. I don't have to be at the graduation ceremony do I? If I am not there he can just put it away and I can get it later."

The response was calm and considerate but clear. "No Elaine. Attendance is required. Only in the event of an emergency is this requirement waived. And that emergency must be very authentic."

Elaine was having trouble catching her breath. "I need to. . . ah, are we finished with these papers?"

"Yes, it appears so. What's wrong Elaine?"

"I need to run, to keep an appointment. Ah, my doctor will get back to you about. . . . about the name thing at graduation."

It was late afternoon and as she hurried across campus Elaine became aware of the return of an old reflex which had long been dormant. The sensor was on and she was scanning once again, quickly noticing large trees behind which someone could be hiding, the double check of that shifty man there walking toward the library. Aware of the movement of leaves on the trees, of the undergrowth in the thick hedges. Aware of that which had slowly receded from her attention, which she had ignored as if it no longer existed. But it did exist. Her new awareness was of the old familiar dread. He was still out there.

* * *

Dr. Keith had always been non-judgmental, a model of patience in the search for understanding. In her class on styles of psychotherapy he was of course analytic, but he also clearly fit the classic profile of the non-directive therapist. So Elaine was somewhat taken aback when he responded to her fear, this time with strong, even controlling determination.

"Elaine, look at me! Look me in the eye. This is the time that good mind of yours simply must assume command. Your fear that the killer will come out of hiding and there, in front of everyone, will kill you as you walk across the stage – that fear is understandably imbedded in history. But it is totally irrational. Keep looking at me and lock in! Elaine, he does not work that way. His M.O. is in the dark, in the night, in poor areas of town. If he is still alive, and we have no evidence of that, he avoids crowds. If he still thinks of you, and we have no evidence of that, he is hardly scanning commencement announcements of Illinois universities to find your name. So on this one, embrace reality. You must do that, beginning now. And for you to reclaim your name bodes well for your new life as Dr. Atkinson."

It sounded like a lecture, but the effect was cold water dashed across her face. And in the emerging clarity she looked at the man who had doused her, and in his strong determination she felt support and affection. He was right; her fear had grown to near panic, fueling the crazy thought that once her name was announced again to the world he would come and kill her. Right there, on stage. And that really made no sense. Furthermore, as she thought about it, if she succumbed to this fear then she would once again be feeding the red wolf.

It was that therapy session which was so grounding for her in the unfolding graduation events. There were several ironies. She had just recently been terrified of the world hearing her name again, but now she was taking the initiative and sending out a dozen "announcements" of her coming graduation. She was Elaine Atkinson again. Of course inviting mother and her competitive sisters to the academic celebration was an invitation for trouble. If only Brian were not so broken and could be here like the comrade he had always been. That thought made her tearful. And then the supreme irony was that she would be receiving her degree on the very stage that Todd was to have graduated just five years before.

The latter was only a passing thought until, on commencement day, she approached the Pavilion which connected Rush University with Illinois-Chicago. It brought her to a complete halt. Over there was the street where Barbara had driven by on their way to the morgue, and she immediately remembered looking over to see the dental school graduates in their caps and gowns, posing for pictures with their families. Todd had only been five hours away from that scene. Tears welled up with the cruel memory. As she searched for a way of coping, the image of the silver wolf appeared, followed by an image of Todd out on the same street, this time watching her in her cap and gown ready to graduate. They had traded places, and the tears became bittersweet.

The commencement ceremony was something of a blur. Once she looked around to imagine the empty chair which the graduating dental class had honored Todd on the day of his death. All in this same room. She caught sight of her family scattered in the balcony, most of them in animated conversation. She would learn later that mother had decided to take Ellen to the bathroom at the very time Elaine would walk across the stage to receive her diploma. It was predictable.

8. The Distant Dream

There were 150 new students in the medical school, and most all of them displayed the effects of the endless grind. Adequate sleep was a long-lost memory. Elaine drank far too much caffeine which left her with a troubled stomach. Classes revolved six days a week and she always sat on the front row of the classroom, a hedge against the humiliation that would come if she dozed off. In addition, student complaints were universal ranging from the sense of being crushed by the weight of incalculable new science information to the sacrifice of personal relationships which the program demanded. Added to this was the oppressive reality of the student loans which promised to keep her indentured into the distant future. And of course any notion of the romance of medical education was quickly eradicated. Embryology and biochemistry simply took the magic out of it all; a full year of the dissections of life turned mystery into data. The human body was becoming a mechanical object.

One exception to this occurred early. It was the established practice that all first year students be assigned to follow a woman through her pregnancy, make a home visit, attend the birth, and then follow the child through the first year of pediatric care. Full medical attention was to be given to new life as well as to the myriad of diseases. Elaine's patient was an African American woman, a single mother with two children, gentle and sweet spirited. The home visit to a blighted neighborhood was disconcerting as Elaine recognized the profound limitations and disadvantages that this new infant would face from its first day of life. Labor ensued on the night before Thanksgiving and Elaine rushed to the hospital, convincing the residents that she should attend. Young Andre was born, strong and vibrant, and Elaine cried at the magic of the moment of delivery. Throughout the first year she would reflect on the bonding she felt toward this mother and child, holding it tight as the restored hope that this relationship with a patient would be the prototype for her future as a doctor.

It was also at this time that Elaine attempted to engage her mother about their ongoing pretensions. Her awareness was magnified whenever mother visited and would interact with Ellen. As she related to Dr. Keith, Elaine would scrutinize her mother for any behavior which even slightly resembled the events of her own childhood. Growing weary with the repression she sat down and wrote her mother a long letter, finally confronting her with the memories of her abuse and recommending family therapy to facilitate any possible healing. Mother's response was dispiriting in its denial and self-righteousness: "I don't know how you could call it abuse. I never abused you. Anything I did was under doctor's orders to examine you for cleanliness." She then wrote a three page letter to Dr. Keith stating that the real problem was the father, that if any molestation occurred he was the offender. She added that Elaine had always been a "horrible child." When Elaine wrote back with the specific details of the reality of her childhood, mother rejected the overture, now arguing of her own victimization. "I gave as much as I received," and "Well, good luck being a better mother. I hope you have a nice life."

Mother's frozen dismissal did bring Elaine to review what kind of mother she was being to Ellen who was now in school, dropped off each morning before work and picked up each evening in the afterschool program. On the occasions of very early rotations Ellen would go to the medical school where she would sit quietly and color. Other students were impressed with how well-behaved and cooperative she was.

Ellen had looked forward to first grade, liked her teacher, and made her first friend. However as the year proceeded she had seemed more withdrawn. Elaine was to learn that the nice teacher was frequently absent and told her students the reason: her mother was dying and it was a difficult time. Ellen had immediately imagined her own mother dying and was quietly and privately afraid. Once this was made public both Elaine and Dr. McQuisition joined in an infusion of reassurance. In the days that followed Ellen progressed as expected, making occasional new friends. But always her most valued time was when she was with her mother. The exception was when being punished with the order "Go to your room." For Ellen this was a momentary sentence to exile.

* * *

The second year of medical school was interminable, an endless blur of study, memorizing, resolve. The vast amount of new medical information seemed limitless and beyond comprehension, overwhelming the energy required to appropriate it. Long days followed long days of demands: learning the metabolic pathways, the schema of pathology, the convolutions of pharmacology. Interspersed were the patient care routines: taking patient histories, giving physicals, taking blood pressures and measurements, assigned with two other medical students to a patient where a doctor would serve as mentor, and sometimes finding a few minutes to listen to patients.

The medical rotations were initiated as the third year began. It was a year which would teach her many things including her strengths and her limitations. She was in the hospital every day learning to do admissions, interpreting X rays and following patients. This was all intimidating not only because of the seriousness of diagnosis and treatment strategies but of the strong personalities of the teaching physicians and nurses. Perhaps there were "margins of error" allowable in the other professions, but not in this hospital. Mistakes, poor judgment, failure to proceed down a diagnostic pathway, and even simple inattention due to fatigue was cause for public reproach and admonishment. Leaving the floor in a state of humiliation was an experience not uncommon to a student.

Her first rotation was six months of Internal Medicine at the all-male VA Hospital. This was a fortunate beginning. Years before she had performed examination grading for the doctor who headed the VA and he remembered her situation. As a courtesy to her life as a struggling single mother, he privately cut her hours from 100 per week to around 70. It was early in this rotation that she was called upon to conduct a complete physical examination on a man, a scenario she had wondered about, then suppressed. Now it was real. And it went well. He was older, a patient she described to others as "a really sweet man", and it was necessary for her to tell him that he had terminal lung cancer. She was deeply touched by how this person, in the very hour of being told of his coming ordeal, exhibited genuine concern for Elaine herself and felt constrained to reassure her that he knew how difficult her job was.

A Family Medicine rotation then followed consisting of office hours eight to five each day with the full array of complaints, disease, limitations, sudden illnesses, and trying to see that patients were compliant with their medications. Elaine enjoyed this two month experience and recognized that if it were not for her commitment to psychiatry this might well be her future specialty.

As she began her next rotation, three months on Ob-Gyn, Elaine had no way of anticipating the near crisis this would produce. She was optimistic and the women experienced her as understanding and her support as authentic. The memory of the mother and child she had followed for two years continued to be instructive. Here was the beginning of life, the vital importance of the strong and confident mother, an essential counter to all the emphasis on disease and pathology which otherwise threatened to consume her. And she was delighted upon learning that some hospital in Illinois had begun the practice of playing a lullaby over the sound system whenever a child was born so that all the sick and suffering would be reminded that new hope and promise had arrived.

8. THE DISTANT DREAM

The problem presented itself without warning during her second month. She found some of her co-workers to be insensitive or even callous to the apprehension of women who required pelvic exams. One male intern with no knowledge of Elaine's history compared the examination table to the dentist chair, in both cases the simple necessity of "open wide" for inspection. Elaine's response to him was curt: "A typical stupid male remark." She would, of course, conduct a pelvic exam, being as reassuring as possible. But then came the day and the predicament. The patient, visibly tense and frightened, tried at first to cooperate. But the procedure was painful and somehow overwhelming. Pushing Elaine back, she cried "No! Stop! That hurts! Don't!" Elaine's response was immediate: "Of course. That's okay." Quickly the situation was brought to the attention of the senior resident and then the attending. They instructed Elaine to continue, that the examination was necessary, that there were some women who simply had to endure very brief discomfort. But Elaine found herself unable to follow these orders. She was criticized by the attending, then dismissed for the day for being non-compliant.

Dr. Keith's schedule was completely filled for the day but he was able to listen to Elaine's call for assistance. He left her a message: "I am going to call the attending. I will need to tell him of your own history of being abused. So call me and leave a recording giving me permission. I will support your need to claim this limit. There are precedents in medical training where for reasons of personal history the intern is to be excused. I know about some of them and will appeal to the dean if needed."

Her final month on Ob-Gyn was, predictably, stressful. Neither the attending nor the senior resident were understanding and remained highly critical of what they considered to be Elaine's unreasonable fear of being intrusive with female patients, or her "neurotic" need to be seen as overly kind. The attending took a parting shot at her in his summary remarks for her record: "She would make a far better midwife than to ever be considered for Ob-Gyn services."

* * *

If Dr. Keith had prevailed in his contention with the Ob-Gyn doctors, the fallout was far from resolved. Elaine was left with some serious misgivings about any other limitations she might have. She was aware that she had avoided autopsies. She could work with her cadaver which was an inanimate specimen, but the body on the pathologists table was just recently alive, and she immediately associated with Todd's body on the table at the morgue. Having to watch them open the body and remove all the organs was sometimes just too much. And this prompted her awareness of the coming rotation in surgery; the setting would be at a Level One Trauma Center well known for treating not just victims of accidents and sudden illness but also the violent world of criminals and street life. And as if this anxiety were not enough she began to become aware of pain in her right eye and periodic double vision. Added to this was her noticing the slight tremor in her right hand that would occasionally appear and disappear. She ultimately dismissed this as likely the function of the constant stress and chronic fatigue. But she was uncertain.

The surgery rotation at Rush was even more intense than she anticipated. She was immediately signed up for eighty to ninety hours per week for the following two months. But she could not complain as all of this was for good reason: the emergency room at this trauma center never stopped. The hospital was at the epicenter of metropolitan Chicago, routinely receiving patients too gravely injured or too critically ill for other hospitals to manage. And it was the gunshot wounds, particularly those gunshot wounds to the head, which were so terribly difficult for her. She could not bring herself to tell the attending about her history or her feelings. Nor could she absent herself from these cases. After her bad experience in Ob-Gyn a second refusal to perform might be cause for her dismissal. Her only recourse was focused determination and perseverance.

But there were so many. It seemed like several times a week, mostly nights, she would meet them in the ER, or follow them for neurological work-up, or to surgery, or study them in intensive care. The world began to appear like a war zone where shooting people was common. One gross head wound was remarkably similar to what she tried not to remember about Todd, but in her act of suppression she only produced another sudden fear. The killer was always out there, and what if he was the one who shot this patient? Would he come to the hospital to erase the surviving witness as he had attempted to do after he shot Todd and Brian? Or what if he were to come in as a patient, himself shot, and she would be required to work on the team who was attending him?

That thought, that this was the kind of place where he might appear, as victim or assassin, precipitated an implosion. Within minutes the unsteady terrain seemed all too familiar. Her deep anxiety was morphing into a dreaded panic state. Her breathing became quicker and more shallow, her focus blurred. When she stepped back from a patient a nurse saw something was wrong. "Are you sick?" Elaine tried to shape her answer correctly but the words just came out. "I feel freaky about some stuff." To her surprise the nurse offered the perfect response. "Hey, it's okay. Go take a break. We all get besieged once in a while. You will be okay." And then the nurse returned to her work with no sign of alarm. And that was the key. If this experienced nurse was so familiar with the ragged edge that she too could be intimidated, then just maybe Elaine's response was not so uncommon. She scanned the ER, observing the intense activity and high energy required of all her co-workers, and began to connect with them in a new way. They were all similar, everyone doing their best in spite of their various limits.

* * *

The fourth year now provided her the opportunity to choose elective rotations. She of course chose psychiatry. Elaine had eagerly anticipated this experience but was totally unprepared to learn that she would be working at the same psychiatric unit where she had been treated as a patient three years before. She immediately wanted to protest this assignment but Dr. Keith cautioned against it, reminding her that she had used up her privilege in the earlier conflict over Ob-Gyn, and any further negative attention would not be in her interest. And besides, he added, that would the setting where she would receive the most expert supervision in the area of her chosen specialty.

She had hoped that new personnel would not know about her or history. But the first morning when she arrived for orientation she noticed that the staff bulletin boards displayed the pictures of the new round of medical students, interns and residents. Several of the former staff recognized her name and face, and the story quickly spread. It was a major stressor for her. Some persons, including the head nurse, were degrading in their attitudes, shaking their heads that someone previously psychotic would now be working as part of the psychiatric team. "The blind leading the blind" was a metaphor she heard on two occasions. But the majority was kind and supportive, and there were no references to the murder of her husband. All that was known was that she had suffered some post traumatic episode.

On the second day she did encounter the same Imogene who was still working as a nurse's aide. Imogene's immediate smile was just as Elaine remembered it, and her kindness just as sincere. Elaine inquired about others. It seemed that Mr. Boggs was out on medical leave, having fallen from a ladder and seriously damaged his hip. And, most sadly, she learned that Inez had just last year resigned from the unit for private reasons. The word was that she had moved to Arizona to supervise art therapy at a private hospital. But little more was known.

* * *

8. THE DISTANT DREAM

Her internship was busy structuring her new role and assignment. For a full year she would be returning to the same rotations but now with increased responsibilities and with the task of supervising medical students while she, herself, was being supervised by senior residents. She would look back, years later, and remember this as the year she truly "became a doctor."

Elaine found her psychiatry rotation to be both demanding and profoundly stimulating. All of her undergraduate studies in psychology were now framed in the most realistic paradigms. Sitting in on case reviews and observing the senior residents and attendings as they formulated diagnoses and decisions for treatment only served to open up new vistas of understanding the complex human mind. She could enter the world of the patient through many different doors: appreciating the developmental history of the person, or the function of the Unconscious, or stresses which had become too great for normal coping. At night she would review the faces of the day and the stories: the grief, the rage, the fears, and sometimes the raw courage. And then she would come to a halt upon learning of some terrible trauma which had at least temporarily broken this person's spirit, or of terrible decisions or habits which had resulted in major destruction. And when she would look upon some patient who had finally become resigned to fate, who had apparently lost the ability to fight back, whose apathy and sense of helplessness was so final, she was perplexed. Why were some finally defeated while others were determined and persistent in hope? And this, of course, led her to reflect upon the mystery of her own resilience. What was the source of that?

* * *

There was an old adage that the mortality rates of hospitals increased in the early months when the new interns and residents were emerging. And Elaine could believe it.

Mistakes were made, information was skewed, fatigue effected memories, sometimes leaving the attendings at their wits end. But that was the origin of the word "patient": poor souls who had to patiently endure the learning curve of impatient young doctors.

It was during this year that Elaine first took notice of the difficulty she was having completing charts at the end of her shift. Her concentration was unsteady. Then came pain again to her right eye which led to diminished or double vision. She brought this to the attention of Dr. Keith who did observe that the pupils in her eyes were not the same size. Upon further examination she reported experiencing numbness in her shoulder and periodic bowel and bladder problems. He diagnosed her symptoms as psychosomatic, her stress exacerbated no doubt by her forthcoming final examinations. She was not at all in agreement with this assessment, convinced that it had a systemic base. And she was certainly not anxious about her national boards, having already taken the first half with no problems. She left his office irritated, brooding, knowing something was not right. It was a gathering darkness not unlike what she had known before. Her only recourse was to resign herself to the grind, fighting the fatigue and periodic migraines.

But the weeks passed more quickly than she expected, and this was a blessing. Events moved forward. She was pleased to complete her national boards with a 98 percentile, then saddened that there was no one to take her out and celebrate. There would be no graduation ceremony until June as she moved immediately into her psychiatric residency at the Pritzer School of Medicine of the University of Chicago.

Now it was required that Elaine bring the full application of what she knew in theory into practice as she diagnosed and treated patients. It was every bit as challenging as she had imagined and she was invigorated by the stimulation of it all. She began to think of herself as Janis-faced, one eye focusing on the patient for a comprehensive assessment and appreciation for what was happening with that person, and one eye focusing on her own inner self, how she was reacting to the patient, privately noting whatever feelings she was having, and probing their nature. This became the matrix of her learning which was expanding daily. She observed the interview of a rapist and was astonished, then excited, that he was truly repentant. It had never occurred to her that such a person could have the most profound regrets, and she began to consider, for the first time, the possibility of true transformation. On the other hand was the sociopath who had molested children. He had been in psychiatric care since childhood. His father had molested him, his mother went to prison, then upon her release proceeded to set fire to their house with the kids inside. He was raised by grandparents until, as a teenager, he was arrested for burning puppies. Elaine understood the utter devastation of his personality development, but she was appalled at his existence. The senior resident remarked about the case "He needs an exorcist, not a psychiatrist." Elaine had responded "We should just euthanize him."

* * *

By now her residency could only fall into a category of an endless concentrated challenge. She was engaging the full spectrum of psychopathology and neurologically related cases. She was supervising medical student and interns attending to both children and adults. But the sheer number of patients she was required to treat as a resident distanced her further from the dream she once had of intimately being invited into the inner world of the deeply troubled patient and establishing a relationship where new life could be discovered. There simply was no time for such psychotherapy. If early in medical school the human body had been transformed from a source of wonder into an embryological or biochemical machine, now the soulfulness of human existence blurred into a melange of sorrow, failure, trauma, denial, retreat, rage, and all the bizarre machinations that people design in their attempts to cope with life. Sometimes she would step back, review the current admissions, imagining all the patients coming together and joining hands in a circle of madness, and for a moment felt herself at the center of cosmic chaos. She guarded against allowing this pessimism to be seen as she supervised and trained the interns.

With each passing month Elaine could clearly define the disparity which existed between her original vision of being a psychiatrist and what she was now, in fact, practicing. She had once imagined herself being like Dr. Keith had been with her, establishing a vital relationship with persons going through the slow process of finding the courage to be authentic. But here those connections happened only occasionally or in passing. Her job was to give medical attention to the patient, then recommend to the ancillary team the more personal touch that the patient might require. It was during this phase of her residency that she remembered her internship rotation in family medicine where the physician settled into relationships with patients over the years. And this memory was convincing: that her future would not be in an in-patient hospital such as this but in a community out-patient setting, working and living with people trying to stay out of hospitals.

*　*　*

In the months before the conclusion of her residency Elaine wondered about the "klutsies" that floated around in her vision. She had long adapted to problems with maintaining focus, but now there were added some issues with memory. Problems of logic were a welcome challenge and she experienced no deficit. But sheer memorization which was sometimes required for pharmacology and case histories was increasingly difficult.

Her primary care physician listened to her and recommended that she consult a neurologist. He frankly told her of his concern, that perhaps she was presenting symptoms of either multiple sclerosis or myasthenia gravis. Elaine then consulted with the neurologist but he dismissed these possibilities. She was greatly relieved. But as she left the office she had a specific memory of the time her obstetrician kept saying that the baby would be just fine, and all the while she knew differently. When Ellen was born, weighing just 3 pounds, 14 ounces, she had no choice but to tell that doctor "this baby was obviously not doing just fine."

* * *

During the final year of her residency Elaine had been moonlighting in nearby regional hospitals. And so upon completion of training it was quite natural for her to make herself available for full practice as a community psychiatrist. Her colleagues at the University of Chicago wanted her to stay and join them. But her decision was clear. Offers came to her from areas which were desperately underserved in psychiatry. Community mental health would be devoid of the more prominent patients she had encountered at Chicago, but here in the reaches of central Illinois, a place of farmers and workers and small towns, she would establish her practice. Her circuit would come to include Peoria, Bloomington and Decatur.

These communities often wanted to publicize her important contribution and asked for a picture for the regional newspaper. Her reaction to the picture was instantaneous: he was still out there and the sight of her face just might bring her back onto his radar. But the news publicity she could not deny. Maybe he would not read the fine print of small Illinois newspapers referring to mental health services.

Events progressed easily and quickly. She found a home for herself and Ellen near Bloomington. It was outside of town, an old farmhouse which welcomed attention and minor repair. Stray cats soon appeared to the delight of Ellen.

And her practice was full from the first day. She was determined to spend quality time with her patients and not rush them through brief medication reviews as some of the agencies wished. These were good people, "good souls" as she said, and they deserved not only medical attention but the most personal care. Already she was scheduling certain patients weekly with the clear intention of seeing them indefinitely if required. There was Beverly Hall for example. This woman had not responded to previous treatment for long term depression. As a nurse she had injured her back lifting a patient and found herself slowly addicted to pain medication she would secure for her own use. Elaine was to discover that the profound shame Beverly experienced in the discovery of her addiction was redoubled by the therapists at a rehabilitation center who were employing "tough love" confrontational techniques. But in Elaine's office she was finding a safe place where she was respected and patiently assisted in the many months that would be required to rebuild her self-esteem.

And then there was Aaron Dawson. This 34 year old truck driver announced in his first appointment that Elaine was his last resort. He had seen previous psychologists and psychiatrists who had interpreted his behavior patterns for him and simply wanted him to revise his thinking. But how could he revise his thoughts if he failed to understand them in the first place. In his desire to find a life partner he wanted insight as to why he would meet a perfectly eligible young woman only to ultimately disqualify her for some shortcoming. If she were intelligent, kind, generous, and genuine she would be insufficiently attractive: pretty but not outstanding. But if she had the stunning figure and the perfect face, he would be mesmerized until her character flaws became evident and he would end it. And so his dating patterns had become serialized, a repetitive pattern of disappointing episodes. Some of his friends admired his prowess, calling him an impressive "player" in the social scene. But he hated that as he did think of himself as "scoring" but of being immature.

8. THE DISTANT DREAM

With Elaine, Aaron was making a connection to help him pursue his insight, beginning to revisit his developmental years when he felt so dismissed by the "in-crowd" at school. Many hours of psychotherapy lay ahead as he would seek to comprehend how he was trying to work through old unfinished business. Only then would it be possible to revise his thinking and re-invent his life.

It was already a growing list of "good souls" who would need intense and frequent work. There was Edward, the minister of a large church, whose Obsessive-Compulsive Disorder was being reinforced by some perfectionism in his own theology with crippling effects. Or Amanda, the sweet graduate student, whose eating disorder had never been resolved in therapy and was now again progressing. Or Kevin who had internalized all the stresses of his family farm into a range of troubling somatic complaints: stomach, balance, fatigue, and sleep deprivation. He would need ongoing attention. Like so many others he needed much more than a brief periodic medication review.

* * *

In 1997, Elaine received a communication from Brian in Detroit. He was having trouble with his arm and there was a rapid progression of symptoms which sounded like Multiple Sclerosis. He went to a neurologist who confirmed this diagnosis but also suggested an even more dreaded condition, mitochondrial disease. With this information Elaine consulted another neurologist who examined her, ordered an MRI, and then clearly identified MS plaques. However he minimized these and reassured her that her condition need not progress. As she left his office she was aware that, this time, unlike the others, she felt relief. This time the old shadow of doubt did not present itself. Life was good.

Over several summers Elaine had rewarded her ever-patient daughter with a vacation trip. They had laughed and talked their way across the country on a train from Illinois to California. They had gone to see the wonders of Grand Canyon. This summer the trip was to Space World in Florida. This would prove to be the best trip ever. At Space World Ellen's excitement and response to the stimuli was a delight to behold. She was fully engaged intellectually, sensually, and emotionally. In the months and years that followed she would be an avid follower of the plans and achievements of NASA.

* * *

Sometimes, driving home after a long day at the office, Elaine would think of Dr. Keith, imagining his day at the office and how different it was from hers. She was with him for what, for fifteen years. How many hundreds of hours? She once had a dream of a practice like his, the long, slow, intensive work over time with a person building or re-building a life. She would not have opportunity, nor energy, for that kind of psychotherapy. But she would be able to know some of the same people over a period of time, being their family psychiatrist. And for some of them she was already feeling a strong attachment.

Attachment. Was this what Dr. Keith felt for her? He never mentioned anything like that, careful as he was to be professional and objective. But he had been there for her, and she knew that what happened to her truly mattered to him at a deep level. And with that Elaine would begin to review, once again, the long journey from the time their work began. The murder. The flight. The full blown syndrome, now called PTSD. The disclosures about her family. The hospitalization. Inez. College and medical school. She had a distant dream and all along he held her to it. That review always left her feeling truly grateful and humble, and she was eager to get back to the offices and help others believe in themselves. She was blessed.

8. THE DISTANT DREAM

Yet on this day in 1998 she did not feel so blessed. She was having another day of feeling totally out of focus. Earlier, she simply could not remember a patient she had treated just two hours earlier. Now she was sitting across from another patient whose name and face was familiar but whose case history was completely outside her memory. This had happened before, particularly when she tried to remember side effects of combinations of certain medications. But today was very frustrating. She blamed it on the migraines that had lasted the previous three days with subsequent sleep deprivation. But the old shadow of doubt returned and she knew something was not right. And so it was that she picked up the phone and called Dr. Steiner, the neurologist at Rush. He scheduled her for complete testing the following Wednesday morning.

She arrived early, eager to get more clarity on her condition. The procedures and subsequent evaluation took up most of the morning. Dr. Steiner then came to meet her and they went to a private office. He seemed uneasy, as if burdened by news that was less than good. Finally he looked up and said in simple terms "You should start phasing out your patients over the next month."

Elaine's denial was immediate and understandable. But she also could read the neurological data, and it was clear. The MS plaques were progressing to a serious level, and now there was reason to believe that her difficulties with muscle weakness and pain and periodic problems of motor control was the result of deteriorating mitochondria.

This was a medical reality. Dr. Steiner was deeply moved, truly sorry. He had even taken a bit of time to search for the name of a medical disability attorney who could help Elaine with the financial complexities of a more limited practice. She needed time. Time to comprehend this unfathomable, inexplicable, absurd turn of events. But the disability attorney called, cancelled an appointment and arranged to see her immediately that afternoon.

On her way to the attorney's office Elaine imagined that she would need to begin to understand levels of limited disability, the sources of any funding, and choices she would ultimately need to make. She found the office building and a parking place, then his name on the lobby register. William Brockman. 14th floor. She already felt queasy from skipping lunch and the prospect of an elevator caused a momentary hesitation. Then the deep breath, the familiar persevering step forward, and the door opened into his suite of offices.

A receptionist came to meet her, calling her by name, escorting her down to the corner office. She inquired if Elaine would like coffee, tea, water. Elaine declined, prompted by another queasy wave.

William Brockman stood as she entered the room, shook her hand, motioned to a large leather chair, and she sat down ready for a conversation. It was not to happen. He had a medical file which had been faxed to his office, now marked by paper clips of notes from his studying it. He spoke words of utter devastation: "This new data immediately invalidates your malpractice and nullifies all of your contracts at the community mental health agencies. So you have two choices. Quit today or quit the first thing in the morning."

9. Epiphany

A sudden snow had jammed the morning freeway traffic causing Dr. Stuart Walsh to be running a bit late as he finally made his way across the Ohio State University parking lot to his office on campus. Thursday was always over-scheduled because of his graduate lecture, reviewing clinical coverage for the coming weekend, his seminar with the residents, and as Chairman of the Department of Psychology his weekly briefing with the Dean. And of course there were his patients who required his full attention. He took off his boots in the hall, shook off his coat, and opened the door. He was surprised to find his secretary, Elise, already multi-tasking.

"How did you get here this early?"

She looked up playfully with that smug smile. "The old faithful city bus. Walk three blocks from the Short North condo to the bus stop and no impediments."

"I know, I know. You don't need to tell me again. The price I pay for quaint suburban living."

"You are sporting a nice suburban sweater though."

"Are you being facetious? You really think I look portly."

"No really. It's very classy. You look hale. Did you pick it out or was it Christmas homage?"

Pleased. "I bought it, thank you."

She nodded, tit for tat. "And I bought the premium coffee this morning for a change. I added two bucks from what was left at the cash bar Tuesday."

"Nice start on this day."

"And here is what your Thursday schedule looks like. Maybe twenty minutes for some kind of lunch."

"Thanks. No time for lunch helps my weight-loss ambitions."

"Just the opposite doctor. Anyway you were behind schedule so I pulled the file for the dean, for the residents, and your scheduled patients. And also you had a call from a Dr. Paul Harris who just wanted five minutes with you this morning. I am trying to remember who he is."

"Paul? Oh yes. Paul is an old friend and colleague. An existential therapist in very private practice for many years. We go way back together."

"I don't recall you ever mentioning him."

"Really? Well, our professional paths are a bit different. Paul is also an Episcopal priest. And he also teaches psychology at the seminary where he is an occasional celebrant."

"Yes, you two are different."

"Maybe. Maybe not. Just after I joined the faculty here he did a post-doc. I got to observe his expertise on establishing therapeutic relationships. Really uncanny. Like no one I know. Then we started running groups together and really got in sync. Even did some at professional conferences. When we did a seminar together over here on Joseph Campbell the students found his theological perspective very stimulating. And that was the beginning of my taking modern theology more seriously."

"Interesting."

"You would like him. But I wonder what he wants. I really would like to get back to him."

"If he literally means just five minutes I could call him and have him drop-by at 10:30, just before your Residents seminar."

"Perfect. Hmm, I wonder what's up?"

*　*　*

Elise had sent Paul over to the conference room, but not after first submitting him to some kind of visual scrutiny.

He pondered. "Was she protective of Stuart for some maternal or even more caring purpose? Or was she checking me out?"

The latter thought bolstered by the free time of waiting for Stuart allowed Paul time to conduct a rare reconnaissance of his public presentation. A mirror down the hall beckoned him and he stood for review. Not bad. Tall, still upright in his six foot height, face tired but sparkling with a slight smile, salt and pepper hair with beard carefully attended each morning. Blue sport jacket and tan slacks, open shirt, preserving the vestiges of a preppy look. No glasses yet. Could it be that she found him, if not attractive, at least interesting?

The door opened and Stuart interrupted his pleasant reverie.

"Paul, to what do I owe this visit?"

They grasped two hands on two hands, an embrace considered but negated in the uncertainty of the moment.

"When Elise told me you were coming over I was both delighted but also a bit alarmed. So the latter first. Is there something wrong? Are you okay."

A large smile of appreciation for the concern. "Oh yes. I am just fine. Keeping up with the pace."

"You look great! Still running marathons?"

"A couple of times a year. And are you still the aspiring golfer?"

"A losing cause. But an excuse to wander through the great idyllic fields."

"Go for it."

"So Paul, Elise says you come over for just five minutes? What is it?"

He reached for his parcel, a large file wrapped in a plastic grocery bag. A moment for play. "I wanted you to have this. Kroger's had a special buy on pork chops and I thought of you."

Stuart looked bewildered.

Paul retrieved the file. "A feeble attempt at humor. Actually this is quite serious. Stuart, I want your consultation on a case."

"What is it?"

"No. No time now. Here is the complete medical file, several years of psychiatric treatment. The medical history in the file is sketchy and tedious, so I have compiled a four page summary of her history. Her story and her treatment and her response."

"This is unusual. Is she STAT or are you in trouble?"

"Just read it. You will find it, ah, most unique. And I will have very specific feedback I want from you. It is important."

"Unprecedented from you Paul. Such a mystery. Is it urgent, like tonight?"

"Oh no. This has evolved over a long period of time. It is, shall we say, a complex case. What I need is for you to find a blessed hour, dive into the file and history, and then arrange for a time with me to discuss it."

"Paul, why is this so special?"

"Read it and you will see."

* * *

"Stuart, you really should not have gone to all this trouble. The Faculty Club no less."

"Hey, I wanted to take you to dinner but you kept saying we needed a quiet place to focus and talk about the case. And now that I have studied it I understand your sentiments. So this is a private room we can have, and here are some snacks, and here is a bottle of Makers Mark. That should inspire us."

Paul was touched. "Well Mr. Hospitality, with this we could solve most any dilemma."

"So, tell me what you want from me."

"O.K. Let's see. First Stuart, just give me your impression of Elaine Atkinson."

A big sigh. "Lord, I can't compress that into a few words. Let me just free associate." He mused as he poured himself a drink. "A truly remarkable woman. How did she even survive such trauma? If she did survive. One blow after another, any one of which might have decimated a normal person. From childhood to the murder. Extraordinarily soulful. Also disquieting. Apparently she was quite lethal before going through that turning point at the hospital. Exceptional therapy, so rare these days. Then medical school. She must be pretty bright, and incredible perseverance. Such courage. All by herself. And then the God-awful descent into MS and mitochondrial disease. And her career cut short in four years. Really tragic."

Nodding. "You reference her exceptional therapy and the turning point in the hospital."

"Yeah. Richard Keith in Chicago. I have heard of him but his is a vanishing breed among psychiatrists. Economics now forbid such painstaking personal analysis. What do we have in Columbus now, one or two psychiatrists who still do intensive psychotherapy? And that only for short term. But Elaine and Keith did great work together."

Paul nods. "Anything else?"

"Well, I had some trouble with this splitting of good and evil which Keith apparently supported. The red wolf and the silver wolf. That seems to have helped her but it is a faulty paradigm. A polarized cosmos with the archaic, primordial battle between Good and Evil. Not even monotheism, but now the Good God verses the Bad God."

"Good point. But hold that one. We will come back to it, and when we do rather slowly."

"Sounds mysterious. But you asked for my impression. Now, of course, I want to hear all about your experience with her. What brought her to your office? How did that happen, and when? And what is this all about?"

Paul studied his drink, then rose and walked around the room, searching for his focus. "Hmm. Well she came to see me in 2003. Referred by her neurologist for some behavioral work with her anxiety. Mild clinical depression. Really just resignation to her situation. Residual PTSD with only occasional references. She was burdened by her weight gain from steroids, by ongoing parental concerns for her daughter, by the loneliness and emptiness of it all. However, it did not take long for our connection to develop. I was to learn that she had been blessed with a profound therapeutic relationship which facilitated a transformation, and with me she could continue with her work. At any rate the more she took me into her story the more I realized I was in the presence of an extraordinary person, although I did not know why. There was something about her drive, her determination, her refusal to surrender. And when her history began to unfold I was astonished. Then almost speechless. Then intrigued. She had experienced a ghastly, unbearable catastrophe from which she could only cope by dissociating into some kind of 'wormhole.' I clinically understood her dissociation at that juncture, but then came her treatment at the hospital and the notable paradigm provided by the art therapist. What you just called the splitting of good and evil, the red wolf and the silver wolf. Somehow this grounded her and she found her way into medical school, and by her blessed DNA managed to traverse that endless field we know so well. All the while in a committed and unwavering therapeutic relationship which saved her. Then her successful residency followed by the dastardly blow. Four years of practice and it is all over."

Silence followed as Stuart studied Paul, then his own sense of unease. Finally he frowned and sighed. "Almost fifteen years of work, to get all the way back and then to have it shattered. Makes me more than sad. Cast down. And I don't even know her. Hmm. Remember when Henderson scrambled back to make it all the way through his residency, then wipes out alone on a midnight highway? Just like that."

"Yeah. Henderson was taken away suddenly, the apocalyptic thief in the night. But hers was an insidious inner deterioration right there at the core of the very spirit which she had resurrected."

"You are waxing theological."

"Well, the very life she had sought to reclaim was now taken from her. Again."

"Yeah. So, how did she cope?"

"She had to face her disability, the reality of no longer working. Living in a little farmhouse with her daughter and some cats."

Stuart measured his next responses carefully. "So, Paul, always the question: who is she to you? Let me guess. Given your long time interest in the research on resiliency, she certainly qualifies as a cover model."

"Yeah. You have to admit, a classic textbook case. How did she survive all that? All of the insults over the years, the anguish, the losses, the lethality, the very endlessness of it. It seemed never to end."

"But it did end. It is over now for her. She is retired. And I can only imagine that this creates conflict for you."

Paul was unclear of the inference. "Say more."

"Look. You have always had this soft spot for people who never quit. If they stay in there and refuse to give up, they win you over. You bond with them. You and Sisyphus."

"So?"

"So what does it do to you that, after a lifetime of determination, she retires in her 50's?"

"What is this Stuart? You think that people don't have a right to stop working?"

"Of course. But for you they don't have a right to quit."

"And what is she supposed to do, Stuart? Her disability is extensive."

"In your mind she is to keep pushing the big rock up the hill even though the situation is absurd. And to create meaning out of the absurdity as Camus contended."

Paul smiled with the increasing clarity of it all. "Maybe she still is."

"Meaning. . .?"

"She is no longer living on the farm with her daughter. Her state of mind is now worlds apart of what it was when I first met her."

Now it was Stuart who rose and paced the room, at first perplexed but gradually irritated by the mystery spinning around him like a web.

"So, Paul, this is suddenly like a game. I am supposed to guess the secret word or something."

"No Stuart. I am sorry. I wanted to take you along in this case in the same manner it evolved for me. And you are right. When I first met her I was saddened not just by her grievous loss but at how after all of that work, almost epic in scope, she was now removed from the very field of battle which, for all its agony, provided her with the exact courage which gave meaning to her life. I framed our connection, just listened to her. I think she found in my understanding a compatriot, someone to literally stand under the loss with her."

Paul stopped, opened another file and removed some papers. "Maybe this will explain it, just as it happened to me. It was maybe a year down the road when, without notice, the breakthrough occurred. But here, take a few minutes and read this. It is in her writing."

My neurologist had referred me to Dr. Paul Harris, a psychologist in Columbus, for some depth relaxation work. We went through that routine and in the process I found it was an excellent therapeutic contact. And so I began, again, to carry forward.

We had worked together for maybe a year when the event happened that changed everything. It was 2004; I remember specifically because it was the week of the anniversary of my wedding. On the previous Sunday at a little church in Granville the discussion had turned to the question "What is unforgiveable?" To me this was a no-brainer. On that dark night in Chicago I had looked into the face of evil which ended my marriage and almost destroyed me. Such evil cannot be forgiven; it must be obliterated.

The event came during a particular therapy session which started poorly and then became convoluted. I had arrived already feeling wretched, depressed for having been harsh with Ellen on some routine things. Then the anniversary prompted me to remember all that I had lost, and this was followed by mother's familiar theological indictment still ringing in my ears: "In life you get exactly what you deserve." I thought I had worked through that condemnation, but here it was back again. This in turn prompted the recitation of my list of sins which, as always, took me back to the bottomless pit of guilt I have about Ellen. How she was launched into chaos even before her birth. How inept I sometimes felt in the first years of her life. How my thoughts of actually killing us both were so horrendous that Dr. Keith had me immediately hospitalized. How in my recovery she tried and tried to comfort me but when my despondency continued she fell into her own depression. In my long recovery and in my return to school God knows I tried to be a good single mother. But so often she appeared lost to me. Lost in my struggle to live. So now in the context of the question at church it took appalling shape. Here was the nadir of despair and I had to say it out loud: "Which is worse? Killing a stranger as the guy did in Chicago, or failing someone you are supposed to love and nurture, which is what I did? For me Todd's death was God's punishment. His sin was loving me."

But then came an absolute turnaround. I remember leaving that session feeling incredibly light. To this day I can't explain what happened. Dr. Harris, I knew, was also an ordained clergyman and a professor of pastoral psychology at the seminary. Although his work was always clinically disciplined I remember thinking of him as a kind of spiritual midwife. But he never directed the discussion to religion or ever preached at me. I would not have tolerated that. Still I just can't remember that particular session. I don't think he responded to my experience of a vindictive God any differently than Dr. Keith had done. But some kind of new window opened that would lead me to an immense perspective, one more vast and unlimited than I had ever known.

I left that office with words ringing in my head. "Go home, be yourself, do what you need to do." Were those words the echo of his counsel or my own? I don't recall. I know what followed was a kind of fugue state. I am in my house and there is no food. Only a piece of fruit. Then I am at the store and I notice a dozen roses are marked down because one is broken. I sense that I am supposed to buy those roses for some reason. I leave and on the front step is a little girl in a pretty dress, literally dancing in the sun. When I learn it is her fourth birthday I give her the one rose with the shorter broken stem. She is amazed and delighted at her good fortune. And this prompts a memory of the time when as a little girl I was admiring the roses of a neighbor lady. She smiled and told me to go pick a favorite one. I went over and found a perfect red one, as rich as a large ruby.

But sadly mother made me take it back and tell her we didn't need any of her roses.

Then it is evening and I am utterly relaxed. I know that some kind of defining moment is building. I remember being astonished to observe my muscles jerking and experiencing my body as spastic. The thought comes to me that I am being released from bondage, that as the chains fall away my entire physical self begins to reach out and reclaim what had been compressed for so long. I finally center myself in a lotus position and release into a kind of Buddhist meditation. The words begin like a mantra, ancient wisdom seemingly intended for me: "I wish you well." At least initially I say it as a mantra. But mantras are designed to create distance from the commotion of everyday life, replacing it with a secluded and peaceful rhythm. And then I know this is not a mantra. These are my words, and there is an exactness to them, a literal precision of an expression from the depth of my being. "I wish you well." I am astonished to realize that this is a consciousness I have never known before and I mean these words as absolute truth. Before me appear the faces of persons of all sorts, those I have loved and those I have hated. "I wish you well." All is being made new. And then I look out across my city replete with its joy and its anguish, and the words come again. "I wish you well." And slowly I find myself lifted up high to behold my entire country, and I give it the blessing of my life: "I wish you well." And then the great height extends to an immensity beyond description. I embrace the whole planet. "I wish you well." And our solar system. "I wish you well." And the universe itself.

Slowly a response begins to return to me. It is an explosion of consciousness bringing with it absolute clarity and purest simplicity. It is the extraordinary realization that it all makes sense. All that I had consigned to such categories as chaos or the absurd, in the grand scheme of things now makes sense. The American political scene of the hour – with the craziness of Kerry verses Bush – it makes sense in that it is a social ritual that needs to be played out. The ignorance of the society, so widespread and appalling, paradoxically is part of the unfolding process and it makes sense. Even my own family with its bizarre expression is some kind of mysterious helix that has a purpose in its downward spiral.

Now I find myself outside my body, going through some actual wormhole, touring the galaxy. It is inexplicable. I am seeing without seeing, hearing without hearing, touching without touching. Many dimensions are advancing at once in a multiverse, and I can see it from the inside out. It is a webbed tapestry, green but with the colors of all of life. I am aware that the past, the present and the future are intersecting at the speed of thought. I interpret this as the very consciousness of God. And so I ask "What became of Todd? Is there life out there?" What I get back is a distinct cosmic belly laugh. It is the kind of laugh you have when your grandchild asks if you had a pet dinosaur when you were a child.

Finally I am standing in an Infinite library. I can pull any book down and read just three sentences, and I know more in that moment than I ever learned in my life. It is clear: the Infinite God is utterly beyond the comprehension of our finite minds. Our perspective is so woefully limited. The system is too big and complex for any of us to screw it up. We used to talk of a million galaxies which was beyond our finite ability to comprehend. Now we talk of a million universes, a multiverse in which our own universe is no more than one small entity in the endless space. Or the people who probe the microcosm, their discoveries overwhelm our capacity to even think. This grain of salt which feels solid is actually a configuration of atoms orbiting a nucleus at vast distances from one another. And each atom is further composed of subatomic particles revolving and spinning into regions which can only be imagined. Infinity: the unbounded and incalculable.

And so in this grand and immense design it becomes finally clear that what we consider evil is only a passing and necessary phase in an ultimate movement toward perfection. The movement is exquisite in its unfolding magnificence. Oh, it is a prolonged grinding process and its pulverized shavings are all the wreckage of human misery: the terrible sorrow and grief, the agony which is sometimes torturous, the brutality and the carnage. This is the very groaning of creation. But we love it so, even through the smoke, the broken dreams, the wilting flower, the bittersweet partings. We somehow come to recognize that even in our imperfections we are claiming our courage to move toward our own perfection as facets of God, even to become just like Christ, with all the capacities Jesus knew.

Stuart slowly put the document on the table, looked at Paul for a very long minute. Then he picked it up and read it a second time. He put down his unfinished drink.

"Paul, I don't know what to say about this. In fact I don't want to say anything about it right now. This is more than just personal disclosure. It is her sacred domain and it commands full respect. To psychologically analyze it right now would be a desecration."

"I understand exactly. And I knew that you would honor her experience even as you sought to critique it."

There followed another extended silence as both of them labored to bring into focus and then balance their feelings as well as their clinical judgment. Stuart broke the impasse. "I want to step away and just live with it, and live with my experience of you, Paul, and how you are involved in this. Are you O.K. with that?"

"Of course."

"Let's find a time next week as soon as we can. I don't want to delay. I will ask Elise to help us. She will look at my schedule, call you, then get this room reserved again."

"You're on."

* * *

It was the same room at the faculty club where they had met six days ago. But this time the Maker's Mark was replaced by brisk English tea. The need for minds to be sharply focused.

Stuart began. "I made several notes during the week, but they never came together in a nice integration. No differential diagnosis. More contrasting perspectives. The leading thought was to affirm the persistent reality of paranormal phenomena. Our dreams, visions, our uncanny premonitions. Right now one of my residents is reviewing the dialogue of psychologists on the white lights of near-death experiences. We are fascinated by these things and cannot ignore their prevalence. But we do submit them to science and, for the most part, explain them. It appears that the society often frowns at psychology for reducing such romantic marvels to dry equations, but it also expects this of us.

But then there is the mystical, or the religious. Now the questions become even more obscure. Persons report visions and revelations not just of daily phenomena but of other realms beyond our own. Voices now from 'heaven.' Or angels or other apparitions appear. Or someone comes along professing a direct interview with God. But this is your domain Paul, not mine. Your expertise is the psychology of the religious experience. I am uneasy with some of this. Things are upside down here. I should be the psychologist bringing to you the case of a woman with a religious vision and seeking your consultation. So I am not sure what you want of me."

"No Stuart. This 'domain' as you call it confronts all of us. It is about human existence. No one is a specialist in that field. So continue. I really want to know what you do with this."

"Well, if society expects science to ultimately explain paranormal experiences, even though it kind of wants to continue to believe in ghosts and the like, something different happens with the religious or the mystical. Religion circles its wagons around its prophets, the stories from its saints which are sacrosanct, and will even go to war with those who dare to explain them away. And so science draws the line, the reasonable and prudent thing to do."

There was lengthy pause and Paul cleared the air. "Stuart, say what you need to say. At this point I hear your words as a preamble to discrediting, or disbelieving, Elaine's vision."

Stuart was obviously uncomfortable with the moment. "Paul, I am utterly respectful of Elaine's experience. After what she went through it is a beautiful perspective. The world fell in love with Anne Frank for her grace and innocence. I see people who are transported by their prayers from despair to a hope and confidence that they are not alone. But you know all of this. The historic Negro spiritual is music of the disenfranchised which forever inspires us. The visions of our artists soar to heights previously unknown, and without them we would be confined to a world with limited joy and light." He searched for more analogies.

"However . . . ?"

"You detect my skepticism."

"It is apparent. I want to hear it."

"Look Paul. Clinically we cannot ignore the fact that historically Elaine has coped with overwhelming and even devastating stress by dissociating. She describes in detail how she mastered this art of transporting herself from her mother's torture over to a realm outside this one. She employed it again at the hospital after the murder, and at the funeral. And we have no way of knowing how many other times she resorted to this. She called it her 'wormhole'. A choice term. And give her credit for being so creative and determined. Otherwise she might not have made it. But isn't it obvious that with this final crushing defeat the work she prepared for on her long road back is just ripped away from her so that now her only way out is through another wormhole. And that is so richly described in this profound vision. Would that I had the capacity to make my way through such a dark valley with such a spirit of elegance."

"But you interpret it as a complex mechanism of defense, strictly a coping strategy."

"Yes I do. Don't you?"

"Well Stuart, maybe yes, maybe no"

"Go on."

"Of course I see the pattern of dissociations in her life and how she has used it for survival. But a closer look reveals something different about this, her latest experience. Her descriptions of her earlier 'flights' away from trauma were about leaving the destructive scene, seeking refuge, but never about arriving at any specific place other than a realm of colors or images of tranquility. But this vision is highly elaborate in its detail. Now she tours the galaxy and beyond, beholding the macrocosm and the microcosm. There is even personal interaction, the wonderful 'belly laugh' from some form of the Deity when she initiated a conversation. And then the rich, intense, breathtaking description of Infinity itself, and how she is staggered in the realization that our minds have been far too small to comprehend this reality, this multiverse. That is not just a flight away but arrival to another place."

"I am still missing something here."

"Stuart, imagine for a second that as she came face to face with the emptiness and final failure, in some moment of downward spiral she opened up the old wormhole and entered. But this time it took her to a place 'high and lifted up' as Isaiah might say, from where she could gain the bigger picture. It was the bigness of that picture, its vastness, which saved her. Now she could comprehend that what we conclude as the final outcome is in error, that there is far more to it than meets the finite, limited human mind. And she was given the opportunity for that viewing. And then came her epiphany: that evil, which she had seen firsthand in its most monstrous human form, was but a passing stage in an evolving and unfolding design leading to some kind of perfection."

Stuart arose from his chair and walked to the window. Down below was the moving stream of students over the concrete paths leading to their next classes. All were presumably conscious but some much more than others. Some challenging great questions or problems, some driven by emotions that either inspired them or terrified them, and predictably some looking for ways to avoid reality. He gathered his thoughts again and returned to his chair.

"So then, the theologian in you wins and you just disconnect your critique of pure reason?"

"Oh come on Stuart. You know me better than that. It seems that every new class of seminary students views me as a possible apostate when I introduce symbolic Jungian archetypes to replace their literal view of Biblical miracles."

Stuart smiled, his tension slightly relieved. "I would like to observe that sometime." Then the seriousness returned. "But Paul, I cannot escape the obvious or apparent fact here, and that is that you believe her. You believe that this was not just a mechanism of defense but that her experience was genuine. Some kind of revelation."

Now there was a long pause as Paul weighed each word, each concept carefully. Finally he sighed: "Well Stuart, what if it really did happen as she says?"

Stuart took a deep breath, frowned, then simply motioned for Paul to continue with his need to elaborate.

"Religious history – and scientific history as well – is characterized by these moments which we call revelations, or epiphanies, or breakthroughs where new depths are revealed. We don't suspend the laws of nature in these moments, but they enhance our understanding. We access the bigger, even more mysterious reality."

"O.K. Paul. But in science we submit the new insights to vigorous empirical testing. Not true of religion, or even psychology. It is all too subjective. A dream is a symbolic three minute story produced by the creative brain, or the voice in the night is an interesting projection of psychological issues. But then someone insists these are messages from beyond."

"Sure. But, Stuart, are you really closed to the possibility that along the way of the journey of human history there have been openings to that realm which are far more immense than we can comprehend?"

"Not closed I guess, but understandably skeptical. And so are you, usually. How can you take this leap of faith?"

"I like the way Paul Tillich put it. He said that we cannot cross the frontier from finitude to infinity. But what he called the Eternal can, from its side, cross over the border to the finite. The Eternal is not limited by finitude. And then he notes that all religions witness to this border crossing."

Stuart was very still. "Let me think about that for a minute." Finally he spoke. "Border crossing. Very provocative. Tillich it seems was forever speaking from just beyond the consciousness of most people. But what does this have to do with Elaine's vision. Are you suggesting that human history was somehow penetrated by her experience?"

Paul measured his words. "Elaine believes that she entered a realm beyond this one. What she discovered there changed not only the way she thought about good and evil but about an evolving process in which we are all facets of God, perfection even in our imperfections. And now she wants the world to know about that revelation. She wants to share her discovery."

Stuart frowned again. "Have you analyzed her grandiosity at this juncture?"

"She doesn't see it as having anything to do with her ego. She dismisses any notion of her being an heroic figure. She simply believes it is incumbent on her to be faithful to the revelation and to pass it on to the world."

"How does she propose to do that?"

"She wanted to distribute a copy of her vision, and to speak about it wherever she could find an audience. I warned her of the great pitfalls to that, that she would be dismissed as just one more street corner preacher, and that most of the elements of her revelation had been previously introduced by others."

"How did she take that?"

"She was not intimidated. But I did say to her that if her epiphany were couched within her own story of such magnificent resiliency, it would be heard with much more credibility."

"So where are you now?"

"Considering finding someone to do the writing. And soon, before her memory dims."

* * *

Two weeks had passed before they met again. This time it was Stuart who called and offered to drop by Paul's office. They could only find a thirty minute break in the schedule.

"Paul, I have gone round and round on this. I am not William James in addressing the psychology of religious experiences. The mystical has its own parameters. Elaine's vision is persuasive in its beauty. But it is clearly a panacea to ward off despair. The bottom has fallen out and now, suddenly, things are so appealing and endearing. It is too neat. Almost psychologically shrewd." He quickly stopped his speech, looking carefully at Paul. "I don't want to be offensive here. She is clearly important to you."

"No, no. Continue. Although I do pick up in your voice something that almost sounds like anger."

Stuart paced again, visibly on edge with the moment. "I am not angry, more precisely I am impatient with what seems to be a contrived, even artificial composition. Look, she is obviously highly intelligent and you would think that she would see her own reach for magic as a solution to her desolation. I mean, come on, to create a fairy tale world where evil does not exist, where we are going on to perfection! Let's take her on rounds tomorrow over in the hospital to the first seventy-five patients who are going through their hell, and let her face those realities."

"Stuart, she is a physician. She has seen all of that. All of it."

"Well then, maybe she can spend the weekend in a patrol car. That comes to mind because I just left a session with a local cop who is way beyond burn-out. One day recently on the job he just shut down. He was called to a broken down apartment, found the mother dead drunk, a naked guy passed out in the bedroom, a two year old crawling around the floor in a day old diaper, an eight year old girl playing some kind of video game, a 12 year old boy smoking a cigarette and just ignoring it all. The cop looked at that all too familiar scene and suddenly concluded that it was already all over for these kids. He knew exactly what their future would be. And the permanent darkness is beginning to descend into his own world."

An awkward silence prevailed. Finally Paul spoke, choosing his words carefully. "Sounds like a soulful cop. But what are you doing Stuart? That scene is this very minute being replicated around the world. She knows that. We all know that."

Stuart frowned, then responded in a tight voice. "She wants to tell the world that this evil is just a passing stage in our movement toward perfection. Not even our major world religions go that far. It is a panacea. And by the way does she wish her killer 'well'?"

Paul sighed. Finally: "She refers to these horrors as the groaning of the creative process. Other mystics have had similar perspectives. But I don't want to debate this. I truly want your critique. You are a tough scientist I can discuss this with who is also a person of faith. I remember when you were working through your Christology and the fundamental concept of revelation from beyond."

Stuart studied Paul, then looked away, reviewing his position on this issue. When he responded his voice was softer. He even smiled slightly. "You have a good memory. My first real Biblical exegesis there on the prologue to the Gospel of John. *En archai ho logos.* In the beginning was the logos – the great creative force, the author of the Big Bang and of all reality that followed. And then the experience of John given to all civilization, that the universe was not just designed by intricate scientific principles but it was also infused with a personal, loving connection and the possibility that we humans could discover that. That the logos became flesh and dwelt among us. Communing with us. Teaching us to love one another. Empowering us in the Eucharist.

That is revelation. That is Tillich's boundary crossing. It changed human history, opening the doors to understanding grace, forgiveness, hope, love, faith. But Paul, you are surely not thinking of Elaine's experience as being in that category, as revelation from the Eternal to the human race?"

"Why not? Some of the Biblical prophets were nameless until they walked on stage. Others were known but as ordinary souls: farmers, shepherds, soldiers, administrators. Truth was revealed through them. Are we to believe that the border crossings have ended? I would remind you that Elaine was not out searching for a word from the Lord. She had no previous mystical history and describes herself as being 'visited' with no advance notice."

"So listen to you. You are thinking of her as some kind of modern day prophet. More than that. She purports to evolve into an equal with Christ. Isn't that rank heresy?"

"To some systematic theologians, probably. Especially traditional Trinitarians who allow for only one Incarnation. But there are many references about 'going on to perfection' not only in the experiences of the historic mystics but in the New Testament itself. Many spiritual traditions pursue union with God even as Jesus did."

"So you are actually open to the possibility that she can be the recipient of direct divine revelation, as Jesus was, to be the manifestation of the Divine nature?"

"I am open to that possibility. That is why I came to consult with you."

Stuart stood up and stretched. The tensions had accumulated more than he realized. He moved closer to Paul, examining his face, feeling a wave of affection for his honesty and his dogged pursuit of spiritual possibilities. He felt that a summation was in order which would require his similar honesty.

"Well Paul, she is a truly extraordinary woman. Her vision, as she calls it, is not just inspiring but mind-boggling. I have read it several times. Her descriptions are deeply grounded in scientific concepts which are so very persuasive. Even beautiful. Hers is Einstein's God, such a far cry from the theological trivia which is common today. And my own emotional responses? A wide range. Joy. Gratitude. Fear. Suspicion. Peace. Hope. Confusion. Impatience. Annoyance. Above all Trust and Respect. I have been deeply touched by her story and will be living with my knowledge of her for a long time.

But I must part ways with you in thinking of her as a modern day Christ, as one receiving the Word from on high which is a message to the people on earth. And I am concerned for her, and for you, if an attempt is made to publish it. I can all but predict the public reaction. Her psychiatric history will only result in general skepticism and misgivings. Prepare for her to be discredited as a crazy woman. Worse will be that it triggers the same contempt from the populace as they have for the crazy leaders of the wild religious fundamentalists, or the hysteric followers of the mindless religious big bands. People today have had enough of the holy prophets, whether those pronouncing *Jihad* in the far East or the radical Evangelicals in the west who claim to have discerned the true will of God."

Paul chose his words carefully. "So you accept the concept of some kind of primary revelation, such as the Incarnation, but that those windows into a reality beyond us are now closed to any new manifestation?"

A long pause. Then he continued. "Let's call it something else besides revelation. We have times when there are discoveries in the science laboratory of realities that have been there all the time but we did not know how to perceive them. Or that our intellectual giants and most inspired spiritual leaders finally interpret a mystery which was previously inaccessible. There is so much we don't know. But it was there from the beginning.'

'Stuart, maybe you and I are closer than we think. I still call that revelation. The core of Christian theology is that God is revealed to us in the most careful study of the sacred Scripture, or in a careful study of empirical science, or in the wisdom of past generations, or in the personal experience of most special illuminators along the way. And when those factors are congruent we have a word from beyond. In a Darwinian sense the unfolding of the ultimate mystery. But maybe the grand design is that there are ongoing border crossings from the Eternal on matters that we have not yet been ready to comprehend. Maybe there are happenings all the time but there are few who can or will receive them.

I need to be open to the deeper messages being delivered in all quadrants of life: the profound observations from the peasant in the fields or mountains; the true wisdom of children at play; the real knowledge animals possess; the consuming visions of artists; the energy field surrounding people at prayer; and, of course, the truth in the creative ravings of a person in a psychotic state."

It was quiet for a long moment. Finally Stuart rose to pick up his coat and to leave. "Thank you Paul. What would we do without people like you storming the temples of heaven?"

They shook hands. "And Elaine. We can't do it alone Stuart. And we need to have people like you investigating the episodes."

Stuart opened the door to leave, then stopped to massage an unfinished thought. He turned to speak. "One more thing. The other night it occurred to me that what I call Elaine's 'discovery' would be much more compelling if, in fact, it not only changed her perspective but changed her life as well. And we didn't talk much about that."

Paul paused, then very slowly gathered his thoughts. "Of course. I should have addressed that. Hmm. How to condense all of that? Well, her perspective, as you call it, manifested itself in her entire new way of being alive. Most immediate was her disdain for material things, what she called 'stuff.' Who really needs these things? Sometimes she called them 'nouns'. In one gesture when her church was having a rummage sale she donated two-thirds of her possessions. A lot of really nice 'nouns' she could do without. On another occasion when her house was flooded she turned it into an adventure. She found it amusing to take a canoe to her front door, and simply remarked 'I need shelter, but I don't need a house.' Those around her described her as 'glowing.' She found it joyful to look out the window even on a drizzly day. She felt true freedom. On one occasion she wrote of her realization that 'it is easy to love your enemy when you discover your enemy is your greatest teacher.' I have that one on file.

So let me bring you up to date. After her experience she remained steady in her sense of being continually astounded by the immensity of her multiverse and her connection to it. Her mother died and that brought a kind of closure. Her daughter Ellen got married and established a new home, bringing a granddaughter into Elaine's life. And then, if you are ready for this, five years ago Elaine was married."

Now it was Stuart who was caught unawares. "You are kidding."

"No, she married an exceptional guy. One in a million. An independent architect who is his own free thinker and disdains the corporate world. They wore tie-dyed shirts at their house wedding, and every guest was required to take something home from their collection of furniture and furnishings. They went through a rough time two years ago when one of his investment projects, an apartment building turnaround, collapsed and their retirement funds vanished. But they bounced back from that, helped no doubt by her view that there were now just fewer "nouns" to worry about. Today they laugh a lot, make love, cook together, raise vegetables and store their harvest or give a proportion to food banks, and devote considerable time working with the poor. Her husband is fully aware of her medical disability and adapts to that."

Stuart was silent, immobile. He examined his disjointed thoughts. "I don't know what to say Paul. I would never have anticipated that. Incredible. It would seem she who was totally defeated is now celebrating her life. Perplexing. A claim of actual transcendence."

Paul smiled. "It would appear so. And one more thing. I still see her periodically. She is as resolute as ever although now short bursts of energy occur within longer interludes of fatigue. And she must sometime struggle mightily. She puts up with pain and dizziness. Her memory sometimes takes flight, but she is good natured about it. Her mortality is certainly impending and I can say I have carefully observed how she faces it with a rather bemused or philosophical curiosity. She exhibits no dread whatsoever. She is absolutely convinced that her transition out of this life will be into the immense design which she has been privileged to preview."

James E. Gebhart, Ph.D., is an ordained United Methodist minister who has practiced psychotherapy for many years as a Clinical Psychologist in Columbus, Ohio.

CPSIA information can be obtained
at www.ICGtesting.com
Printed in the USA
BVHW03s1310120718
521482BV00001B/39/P